EVANGELISM AND MISSION

Evangelism and Mission

Biblical and Strategic Insights for the Church Today

Benjamin A. Kwashi

AFRICA CHRISTIAN TEXTBOOKS

2018

Evangelism and Mission
Biblical and Strategic Insights for the Church Today
© 2018 Benjamin A. Kwashi

Africa Christian Textbooks (ACTS)

ACTS Bookshop, International HQ, TCNN,
PMB 2020, Bukuru, Plateau State, 930008, Nigeria
GSM: +234 (0) 803-589-5328; E-mail: pa@actsnigeria.org
Website: http://actsnigeria.org

ISBN: 9789789053803 Print
ISBN: 9789789053810 ePub
ISBN: 9789789053827 Mobi

Cover Design: Billy Abwa
Book Design: Peter Fleck

CONTENTS

FOREWORD

"The church exists by mission, just as fire exists by burning." This remark by the Swiss reformed theologian Emil Brunner takes us to the heart of what Archbishop Kwashi expounds with so much passion and joy in this book. Mission is not just something that the church is supposed to do. It is the very purpose for which Jesus Christ created it. We are to

> Go and make disciples of all nations, baptizing them in the
> name of the Father and of the Son and of the Holy Spirit,
> teaching them to observe all that I have commanded you. And
> behold, I am with you always, to the end of the age.
>
> —Matt 28:19, 20

This is our great commission. It is no optional extra; it is the very thing that we exist to do.

Few people would be unwise enough to question whether the church should undertake mission. However, there are many who would make that mission something that does not involve evangelism. Even those who recognise evangelism as essential to mission are not always sure how to go about it. This book speaks to both of these groups. Archbishop Kwashi makes clear what mission is: it is both evangelism and social justice – not just one or the other but both inseparably together. How can you speak of the love of Christ to people who are hungry, and not feed them? And how can you feed them without telling them about the love of Christ? Both are expressions of the gospel. Mission always involves word and deed. The first half of this book (Parts I and II) makes that wonderfully clear.

But this book also explains how to undertake the work of evangelism. That is where Part III comes in. Once we are persuaded that we are to be bold evangelists, there are some tried and tested methods that we can use to implement the mission. Here, the Archbishop is unsurpassed. He is able to draw on not only his wide reading but also his deep experience of a lifetime of evangelism. This book teaches you about personal evangelism, preaching evangelistically, and following up converts. It also explains how to organise the church to be doing each one of these. You could justify buying this book for chapter 8 alone, "The Need for a Strategic Approach." Imagine the worldwide Church taking these things to heart and seeing every parish and diocese embark on such a mission? Why not?

Let us remind ourselves again: mission is not one of many tasks a church may undertake. It is central to our existence. As missiologist Tim Dearborn put it, "It is not the Church of God that has a mission in the world, but the God of mission who has a church in the world." So I very much hope that this book will be widely read. It is hard to imagine anyone getting to the end of *Evangelism and Mission: Biblical and Strategic Insights for the Church Today* without feeling an excitement about mission and an eagerness to be "doing the work of an evangelist" (2 Tim 4:5). How amazing that the God of the universe calls people like us into his work of reconciling the world to himself (2 Cor 5:18)! Who would want to miss out on that?

The Very Rev Dr Justyn Terry,
Dean/President and Professor of Systematic Theology,
Trinity School for Ministry,
Ambridge PA, USA.

ACKNOWLEDGEMENTS

This book is the product of our work in Zaria, Ikara, Zonkwa, Kaduna, Wusasa, Plateau and Nasarawa States in Northern Nigeria. The adventures of evangelism and mission in these areas are responsible for forming us and solidifying our convictions while sharpening our focus on the way. We are convinced that the gospel is able to save, to transform, to revive and to build communities while setting them free from bondage, lies, traditions and customs of darkness into freedom in Christ. We have been privileged to be witnesses of what the power of the gospel can do and has been doing in practical terms. We remain eternally grateful to the Lord for sending us to these places, and for inspiring and sustaining us through all the up's and down's. Likewise we express our sincere appreciation of all the many people who have been our colleagues and our partners in God's work in these areas and throughout the world.

What we have learned through experience is what we now record in this book, so that others too may learn. The discussions are transferable concepts and adaptable from one culture to another because the gospel message remains the same wherever in the world we may be. We are saved and called to become involved in evangelism and mission so that those who are then saved will continue evangelism and mission in an unending cycle until Jesus returns.

INTRODUCTION

In the early centuries of the Christian Church, North Africa was a thriving centre of Christianity, producing outstanding theologians such as Origen, Tertullian, the great Augustine and a host of others. Indeed, classical orthodox Christianity can be said to be African in origin. Yet today those churches are no more, and North Africa is now predominantly Muslim.

On 7th September 2001, a girl in Jos, Nigeria, was walking home following the route she had always taken, but on that day, Muslims said she had desecrated their prayers. Days of riots, destruction and killings ensued. Fourteen years later, however, the church in Jos still stands. Why? What has - so far at least - kept us from meeting the fate of those earlier faith communities who are now just a memory?

It is my conviction that the vital factor here is a commitment to mission and evangelism. The North African churches of the early centuries were Roman imports who never reached out to the local people in the surrounding areas. Rather, the churches were often ethnic "social clubs," pleased with who they were and intensely inward looking. History has shown that churches such as this are easily swept away. To make matters worse, these churches were also characterised by division over theological issues, and were more interested in intellectual debate than in genuine, active mission. Therefore, when Islam arrived it met a church already torn apart from within and unable to present any uniform front-line of defence. When priority is no longer given to mission, the church will soon weaken, degenerate and die. We must constantly observe Jesus' Great Commission (Mt 28:18-20), not only because it is his command, but because it is the very lifeblood of the church.

Religious violence, commencing with the historic burning of churches in 1987 in Kaduna State, has been the atmosphere within which much of my ministry and mission has taken place. Reflecting on that I have concluded that I have no choice but to love the world as Jesus loves, and to love the Muslims in Jos as Jesus loves. I am not at liberty to kill anyone. If I were to kill, I would have no one to whom I could preach and show love.

In spite of the trials, the church on the Plateau is still standing, thanks be to God. I am convinced, however, that the moment we lose our passion for mission and evangelism, and the necessary boldness to accompany it, we will fall. It is because of this conviction and because of the urgency of our task that this book is revised, expanded, and reissued. This problem is not just in Northern Nigeria or in areas facing Islamic persecution. In the West, aggressive sensualism and secularism persecute the church in another and sometimes more subtle way. If the church is to have a future and not just a past, we must always re-learn and return to the task of being disciples who make disciples. That requires training and boldness.

It seems today that slowly and steadily, starting from the West but now reaching almost everywhere, there is growing a calculated, definite inoculation against boldness when it comes to the gospel. It is important for believers to know that we need boldness through the empowerment of the Holy Spirit constantly to live out the faith we proclaim, to stand against the forces of evil, to insist on enthroning truth as revealed in the word of God, pursuing righteousness and justice and the promotion of love amongst all people. The boldness to do all these things is totally dependent on our conversion, our continuing relationship with the Lord Jesus Christ, our desire to pursue the mission and ministry of the Kingdom and our commitment and obedience to the Lordship of Jesus Christ in all things and at all times. It is the power of the Holy Spirit that gives boldness to the believer both to proclaim, and to demand a response, to the saving power of the gospel of Jesus Christ.

This work is only a beginning: we can explore mission and evangelism, we can consider how to go about the work, but that is all. To actually DO the work requires a living, active faith and the power of the Holy Spirit: we cannot share what we do not possess. As we read, we must also put our reading into practice. Abstract facts are dead; the power of God is dynamic. It is my prayer that the Holy Spirit will so empower all who read this book, that each may boldly undertake the task Our Lord has given to us all.

PART I

WHY ?

THE TASK

CHAPTER 1

THE STORY

> It is not so much that God has a mission for his church in the world, as that God has a church for his mission in the world. Mission was not made for the church; the church was made for mission - God's mission.[1]

"Oh, mission – again!" said Anna. The disparaging voice, the frown of dislike and the lack of interest on her face were clear. She turned away from the church to look for something more "interesting" to do.

Sadly, this is the attitude of many churchgoers and indeed of some churches. Most will not say so openly, but mission is not a hot topic of conversation, and mission concerns may be relegated to the bottom of the agenda of the Church Council, Committee or Vestry meeting, while the real interest centres upon the repair of the church building.

This is a big misconception! The exciting thing about following Christ is that he calls us to be alive, moving and active – not just maintaining the past or sitting complacently in the present, but positively moving forwards into God's future! Mission, therefore, is not something "extra;" it is not something to be afraid of; it is not something for a select but crazy few. Mission is what the gospel is all

---

[1]Wright, Chistopher J. H., *The Mission of God's People*: Grand Rapids: Zondervan, 2010, p. 17.

about! If God were not interested in mission surely he would never have sent his Son into the world to save the world – and there would have been no gospel!

God's Mission (sometimes referred to by the Latin words "Missio Dei"), is a far larger project than merely opening new churches or attracting a few new members. The vision of this mission is that creation and the whole human race (which has been spoilt by sin) are to be restored! A redeemed humanity, living in a new heaven and new earth, is to be the end result. This is the big scene, the ongoing story, the heartbeat of God. We are a part of this story, and the part we play now will affect the lives of those around us, and of those who come after us. If we opt out, God's mission will continue, but our part will be lacking, and we ourselves may not realise how much we are missing – until it is too late. In a choir, all the voices and all the different parts combine together to make one glorious song. If one choir member is missing, the song goes on and others are caught up in its beauty and its message, but the one who stayed back is left alone and ultimately frustrated.

There are many different voices, many different parts in mission. All are valuable and all are needed. Those who travel far are not more important than those who stay in their own locality; those who preach are not more valuable than those who visit a sick person in hospital; those who welcome visitors at the church door are not more important than those who have already cleaned and swept the floors. God needs all these, and still more, thousands more, in fact everyone! God calls each one of us by name, and in calling, he calls us to follow him, and to call others to come with us. All this he does because he loves each and every one, and does not want to lose a single person.

But now thus says the Lord,
he who created you, O Jacob,
he who formed you, O Israel:
"Fear not, for I have redeemed you;
I have called you by name, you are mine.
When you pass through the waters, I will be with you;
and through the rivers, they shall not overwhelm you;
when you walk through fire you shall not be burned,
and the flame shall not consume you.
For I am the Lord your God,
the Holy One of Israel, your Saviour.

—Isaiah 43:1-3

Beloved, let us love one another, for love is from God, and whoever loves has been born of God and knows God. Anyone who does not love does not know God, because God is love.

—1 John 4:7-8

God the Creator

At the beginning of Genesis, we hear that God created the world, and we find the constant refrain, "and he saw that it was good." Sadly, disastrously, sin entered. Adam and Eve proved to be disobedient – and suffered the consequences of this sin. The story of how Cain in a fit of anger and jealousy killed his brother Abel (Gen 4:1-16) shows the ugly nature of sin, and of its consequences. By Genesis chapter 6, the wickedness was so great that:

the Lord regretted that he had made man on the earth, and it grieved him to his heart. . . . Now the earth was corrupt in God's sight, and the earth was filled with violence. And God saw the earth, and behold, it was corrupt, for all flesh had corrupted their way on the earth. And God said to Noah, "I have determined to make an end of all flesh, for the earth is filled with violence through them. Behold, I will destroy them with the earth." Now the earth was corrupt in God's sight, and the earth was filled with violence.

—Genesis 6:6,11-13

Only Noah's righteousness prevented the end of humanity. After the flood, however, things proved to be no better, with God having to intervene decisively at Babel, to defeat the egoism and pride that had taken root in sinful human hearts (Gen 11:1-9). This is a sad history, and one that reflects so much of modern life: disobedience, violence, pride, arrogance, and all other forms of sin.

Nevertheless, in Genesis chapter 12, God again renewed his world through the call of Abram. The call of Abram was clearly not merely for his own reward, but it was in order to further the missionary purposes of God. In Genesis 12:2-3 God said to Abram: "And I will make of you a great nation, and I will bless you and make your name great, *so that you will be a blessing.* I will bless those who bless you, and him who dishonours you I will curse, and *in you all the families of the earth shall be blessed.*" (ESV, italics mine.) God is clear in his intention: he will not wash his hands of either humanity or creation, and with Abram he set in motion a plan for the ultimate reconciliation of the nations to each other and, by dealing with human sin, the reconciliation of humanity both to God and to the created order.

In Exodus, we see God's establishment of the people of Israel as the inheritors of the call of Abraham. Called to be a holy, "set apart" nation, God's kingdom of priests, the intention was never that they might be glorified, but that God might be glorified, and the light of that glory be reflected to the nations through them. Israel, however, proved to be as difficult as the rest of humanity, turning back to God's ways for short periods, then falling away again and resisting the exclusive call of God. This happened time and again until only a remnant remained.

> 'Thus says the Lord, Behold, I am shaping disaster against you
> and devising a plan against you. Return, every one from his evil
> way, and amend your ways and your deeds.' But they say, 'That
> is in vain! We will follow our own plans, and will every one act
> according to the stubbornness of his evil heart.'
> —Jeremiah 18:11-12

Eventually, the light to the nations did come forth from them, but it came through just one person, Jesus Christ.

God the Redeemer

> For God so loved the world, that he gave his only Son, that
> whoever believes in him should not perish but have eternal life.
> For God did not send his Son into the world to condemn the
> world, but in order that the world might be saved through him.
> —John 3:16-17

God is in the business of saving not just individuals, not just the people of Israel, but also the whole world. That is what God's mission is all about! God's love is so great, so total and so amazing that despite the fact that his people, whom he had called, persisted in preferring other gods, and in blindly following a self-centred road to destruction, he still went out of his way to search for them and bring them back, like a shepherd lovingly and diligently searching for that one lost sheep. The cost was high. It cost nothing less than the life, the rejection, the torture, the suffering and the death of his Son, Jesus Christ. Such was the length to which God was prepared to go in order to save the world. That was the cost of God's mission.

The cost could not have been higher – and the result could not be greater! Because Jesus faced – and defeated – the very worst that the devil could devise, there is now no power which is greater than his power, no evil which is stronger than his strength to save, and there is nothing that can separate us from him. As Paul declared in Romans 8:38-39:

> For I am sure that neither death nor life, nor angels nor rulers, nor things present nor things to come, nor powers, nor height nor depth, nor anything else in all creation, will be able to separate us from the love of God in Christ Jesus our Lord.

We can do nothing to save ourselves; we can never earn a place in heaven by running up a big credit balance of good works. To quote St. Paul again, "For by grace you have been saved through faith. And this is not your own doing; it is the gift of God, not a result of works, so that no one may boast." (Ephesians 2:8-9). We exist in this world because of the love of God in creation, and by his grace, we shall exist in the world to come because of his love in redemption.

It is not that we serve him and run around trying to please him by doing what we do not actually want to do, in order to try to secure our place in heaven! It is, rather, that when we realise the extent of his love to us, personally as well as corporately, our response is that of joy, wonder, love and praise. By his grace, we then put our faith in him and want, yes want, to love and serve him in return. Christ gave his all for us, what can we not do for him!

> Were the whole realm of nature mine,
> That were an offering far too small;
> Love so amazing, so divine,
> Demands my life, my soul, my all.[2]

This is our motivation for mission. This is the gospel we have to proclaim. This is the good news for people all over the world – and in our own back yard. This is God's mission, and it is our mission too.

---

[2]Watts, Isaac (1674-1748)

The Ongoing Story

One of the Eucharistic Prayers in the American *Book of Common Prayer 1979* (a prayer held in common with the Roman Missal and drawn from the ancient Liturgy of Saint Basil) says:

> When our disobedience took us far from you, you did not abandon us to the power of death. In your mercy, you came to our help, so that in seeking you we might find you. Again and again you called us into covenant with you, and through the prophets you taught us to hope for salvation.
>
> Father, you loved the world so much that in the fullness of time you sent your only Son to be our Saviour. Incarnate by the Holy Spirit, born of the Virgin Mary, he lived as one of us, yet without sin. To the poor he proclaimed the good news of salvation; to prisoners, freedom; to the sorrowful, joy. To fulfil your purpose he gave himself up to death; and, rising from the grave, destroyed death, and made the whole creation new.
>
> And, that we might live no longer for ourselves, but for him who died and rose for us, he sent the Holy Spirit, his own first gift for those who believe, to complete his work in the world, and to bring to fulfilment the sanctification of all.[3]

This is the story in which, by God's amazing grace, we are now called to take our own part. It must, however, be remembered that we are all fallen creatures, and before we can become effective agents of restoration and reconciliation, we ourselves must encounter the grace and the forgiveness of God in our own lives. Even then, we cannot just go ahead on our own, but the good news here is that God does not expect or wish us to "do it alone." The gospel is not our story, it's God's story, and the enabling power for telling that story is not ours: it comes from God.

---

[3]*The Book of Common Prayer*, New York: Church Pension Fund, 1986, pp. 373-4.

After the resurrection, Jesus commanded the disciples to go and make disciples of all nations (Matthew 28:19-20), but he also ordered them to "Wait," to wait for God's time and for God's power:

> And while staying with them he ordered them not to depart from Jerusalem, but to wait for the promise of the Father, which, he said, 'you heard from me; for John baptized with water, but you will be baptized with the Holy Spirit not many days from now.'
>
> —Acts 1:4-5

> 'But you will receive power when the Holy Spirit has come upon you, and you will be my witnesses in Jerusalem and in all Judea and Samaria, and to the end of the earth.'
>
> —Acts 1:8

The disciples were witnesses to the life, death and resurrection of their Master and the amazing truth is that what happened all those years ago is not just a historical event: it has a relevance and a transforming power that is powerful today and will be powerful tomorrow and into all eternity. The story of the early church as recorded in the Acts of the Apostles has no conclusion: the story continues. Acts, however, shows that this work can only be done in and through the power of the Holy Spirit; the church was born out of the Holy Spirit and continues through the Holy Spirit. Without the Holy Spirit, we are as useless as a car without fuel. This is true no matter what our human intellectual qualifications, experience or abilities may be. It is impossible to be a true Christian without the Holy Spirit; the Holy Spirit convinces and convicts; He is the Spirit of truth; He exposes sin; He is alive! It is the Holy Spirit who brings power, courage, the ability to preach and to go out into the unknown on mission; He is a transformer. The promise of Jesus to his disciples remains a promise for his church today: *"But you will receive power . . . ."* (Acts 1:8)

The disciples waited, staying together and praying. Suddenly and unexpectedly, they had the most remarkable experience. It was as if there was the sound of wind and the appearance flames of fire (symbols reminiscent of Moses on Mount Sinai and also before the burning bush). They were filled with the Holy Spirit. The waiting time had been crucial. That they were "filled," indicates that there had been an emptiness: this had come from the waiting time when they had become emptied of themselves. Now they were available and able to be filled with the Holy Spirit. The prophecy of Joel 2:28-29 was being fulfilled:

> And afterward,
> I will pour out my Spirit on all people.
> Your sons and daughters will prophesy,
> your old men will dream dreams,
> your young men will see visions.
> Even on my servants, both men and women,
> I will pour out my Spirit in those days.

The coming of the Holy Spirit was a startling heavenly event (*"a sound from heaven,"* verse 2). Some of us want the Holy Spirit to work in our own, known ways. The Holy Spirit is not to be controlled by humans! There was a violent wind: the Holy Spirit is not timid! A strong wind can uproot a tree; the Holy Spirit can uproot a person from where he is and put him where God wants. The Holy Spirit is against all that is against God, and all that is against God will be violently thrown out. There were also "tongues of fire." You do not touch fire with your hands; you do not play with fire. The Holy Spirit will burn away all the dirt and chaff and disobedience of your life. When this fire has taken away all the dirt a fresh boldness will come upon you and you will declare the wonders of God. When you are not filled with the Spirit you cannot oppose sin, you are powerless and helpless.

When the Holy Spirit comes, however, a real change, a significant change takes place. It is a change that removes fear, a change that separates darkness from light. Who were these first apostles? They were just fishermen, local government workers, ordinary family men, but they were people who wanted to follow God; people whom the Lord had told to wait for the Holy Spirit. They waited . . . and in the power of the Holy Spirit, they were transformed into fearless, gifted preachers and teachers. This set the pattern for the rest of their lives.

This same Holy Spirit is still God's gift to us today, as we in our turn pick up the exciting challenge of living for God, and take our part in God's story. Mission is not an optional extra. "Mission" is our way of saying "Jesus is Lord."

Digging Deeper

1.   What do you understand by "Mission"?

2.   How would you describe "God's Mission"? What are the implications of this for the world today?

3.   How important is it that each person involved in mission has a clear, personal testimony of conversion and salvation? Share your testimonies with friends.

CHAPTER 2

THE EXAMPLE OF JESUS

A missionary reached a remote tribe who had never heard the gospel. He stayed with them, learned to communicate with them and began to tell them about Jesus. They listened but were not convinced; they continued in their pagan beliefs and practices. After some years, the missionary returned to his own country thinking that he had failed. A few years later, another missionary reached the same village and began to tell the people about Jesus. Their response astonished him. They said, "Oh, we know that man; he used to live here!"

If we in our turn are to be faithful stewards, committed to passing on the gospel, which has been entrusted to us, we ourselves must first be shaped and discipled by that gospel. We must learn from the teaching and life of Jesus Christ, so that others can see something of Christ in us and in the way we live.

In every moment of his life Jesus lived and demonstrated the mission of God; his whole life was the evidence of God at work in human form. He taught; he lived out what he taught; and he trained his followers to do what he did, thereby enabling them to carry on the mission of God and to pass it on for future generations to do likewise. The effectiveness of Jesus' ministry lay in his ability to teach, to live out his teaching, and to train his followers through practical experience in the field. He never asked others to do what he himself would not do.

> And Jesus went throughout all the cities and villages, teaching in their synagogues and proclaiming the gospel of the kingdom and healing every disease and every affliction. When he saw the crowds, he had compassion for them, because they were harassed and helpless, like sheep without a shepherd. Then he said to his disciples, "The harvest is plentiful, but the labourers are few; therefore pray earnestly to the Lord of the harvest to send out labourers into his harvest." And he called to him his twelve disciples and gave them authority over unclean spirits, to cast them out, and to heal every disease and every affliction.
>
> —Matthew 9:35-10:1, ESV

In these few verses, we are given a neat summary of Jesus' attitude, character and method in mission. Jesus does not just go about lecturing about mission; he leads and shows how to do it! Jesus IS the gospel incarnate! Jesus introduces the disciples to the heart of God and to what is needed to do mission in God's way. Seven things stand out for missionary disciples to take to heart if our mission is to have a global perspective, bring forth fruit and bring glory to the Lord. Jesus' model of training was an apprenticeship/discipleship model. He spends time with the disciples, taking them through the mission fields, talking with them about what is God's priority, and showing them what the work looks like. Jesus is careful to introduce them to what it takes for them to make mission worth the effort and to be fruitful. We in our turn are called and sent to do as he did, to teach as he taught, and to live as he lived.

1. Jesus on the Move

> And Jesus went throughout all the cities and villages.
>
> —v.35a

Jesus went about preaching the good news throughout cities and villages. This is a clear demonstration that the good news is not meant to be static but to be taken to everywhere in the world. Twenty centuries after the life of Jesus on earth, the communication and transport systems available to the church are very different from those that Jesus and the apostles knew. These advances in technology mean that mission must have a truly global perspective. The joys, the problems, the sorrows, the situations of the different regions will vary from one to the other, but the church must be prepared to go, in obedience to the Lord's call, from everywhere to everywhere. A church that is not on the move will soon become a maintenance workshop incapable of producing anything new and able only to maintain old, worn out and dying commodities. Jesus shows the disciples that to be an evangelist, a missionary is to be on the move. There can be no sitting down in one location but one will always be looking out for areas where the saving message has not yet been preached.

2. The Gospel of the Kingdom

> teaching in their synagogues and proclaiming the gospel of the kingdom and healing every disease and every affliction.
>
> —v.35b

Jesus demonstrates the purpose of ministry, that is, to bring the gospel of salvation to people. This gospel is only effectively brought holistically: through teaching the Scriptures, through preaching in order to demand response, through bringing healing to the sick in mind and body, and through welcoming, loving and caring for all people of whatever tribe, sex, ability or background. This is the gospel of the Kingdom, bringing the rule and authority of God to bear over every situation, both spiritual and physical. Our ministry is incomplete unless it comes to people in the same way that Jesus demonstrated.

3. Opportunity to Serve

> When he saw the crowds
>
> —v.36a

Jesus saw the crowds in their true condition. What he saw was not what other people usually see. Many people see the crowd as a liability, a political stepping stone, a bunch of ignorant people of whom one may take advantage and use to attain selfish ambitions. Jesus saw something different: he saw a harassed, helpless and needy group of people who were like sheep without a shepherd. He saw an opportunity to serve in order to bring them freedom, self-worth, healing, direction in life and restoring their humanity in God. Do we see the crowd only for the offerings they will bring? Do we see a crowd and look down on them? Do we look down on a race? Do we look down on a tribe? Do we look down on the youth? What do we see in the areas of our primary calling? What we see will determine how far we go, what we do and how we do it. Do we see with Jesus' eyes or through our own tinted spectacles? This will determine our perspective.

4. Compassionate Ministry

> he had compassion for them, because they were harassed and
> helpless, like sheep without a shepherd.
>
> —v.36b

This is the heart of the matter in Jesus' approach to salvation. In all Scripture, the one thing that moves God to action on behalf of the poor, oppressed and lost is his compassion. Compassion drives action! Loving our brother is part and parcel of loving God. Consider 1 John 4:20-21: *If anyone says, "I love God," and hates his brother, he is a liar; for he who does not love his brother whom he has seen cannot love God whom he has not seen. And this commandment we have from him: whoever loves God must also love his brother.*

Our call to mission is a call to self-sacrifice, to give our time, talents and resources, and to show practical care and concern until the mission work is finished and completed. Mission without compassion is not likely to be in line with the mind of God!

5. Labourers

> Then He said to His disciples, The harvest is plentiful, but the labourers are few;
>
> —v.37

Harvest time is the best time for the farmer. It is a joyful exercise; it is a time of singing and thanksgiving. Why ministry is not joyful is because it is not in line with this text. When our ministry is not harvesting, we find it boring, tiring, and we may even wish to give up.

Jesus showed the disciples the work ahead and made it clear that what was needed at this time for the Kingdom was willing labourers. The world then as now is looking for leaders, chiefs, professionals, and qualified top directors to fill vacancies for any job, even in the church. Qualifications and professional skills are not wrong in themselves, BUT the work of the Kingdom demands that we forget who we are and use all our qualifications and acquired skills for service in the harvest fields. We are not called to do the hard work of farming, we are simply invited to come in and harvest! Nonetheless, this is a task only for those who are willing to roll up their sleeves and make the sacrifices necessary so that they can joyfully engage in harvesting for the Kingdom. It must be stressed that this harvesting is for the Kingdom, and not for our own sake. The harvester is nothing but a labourer. The labourer will receive his reward in due time, but the harvest belongs to God.

6. Pray

> Therefore pray the Lord of the harvest
>
> —v.38a

Here is one activity, which the Lord himself assures us he will definitely honour. We are called to pray earnestly to the Lord of the harvest to send out labourers. This calls into question our recruitment processes for ministry and missions. Our primary concern should be to ask God to send the labourers that he wants for his work. Are the people we put forward a result of answered prayers, or are they brought in to achieve a certain objective for our personal goals? Are we interested in bringing in those who will labour for the harvest, or those who will labour for us, ministering to our needs and to the needs of our families? If we ourselves are engaged in ministry because of the prayers of others, we cannot but trust the Lord to answer our prayers in sending out others to join us. Remember the harvest field is not ours and we MUST consider the interests of him whose field it is. The harvest is no place for the lazy, the self-promoting, or self-serving.

7. Sending

> to send out labourers into his harvest.
>
> —v.38b

The mark of a missionary church is in its sending capacity, and whether it sends its best, most suitable, and most qualified to bring in a bountiful harvest. The one who is sent is sent to fulfil the task of carrying the message. A messenger is only as important as the message he is carrying: once the message is delivered and the task carried out the messenger returns to give a report of the task accomplished. The task of harvesting for the Kingdom is reserved only for those who are sent by the Lord, who are a direct result of answered prayers. The work in the harvest field is not for those who send themselves or who are sent by man, no matter who the man may be.

The disciples watched, worked, listened, learned, followed and lived with Jesus for three years. Finally, when he was about to go back to the Father in heaven he left this command:

> All authority in heaven and on earth has been given to me. Go therefore and make disciples of all nations, baptizing them in the name of the Father and of the Son and of the Holy Spirit, teaching them to observe all that I have commanded you. And behold, I am with you always, to the end of the age.
>
> —Matthew 28:18-20, ESV

This is more than a hint, a guide or a suggestion; it is a command, and the apostles took it very seriously because it was, and still is, the will of the living God. All the things that follow in the wake of evangelism: the social consequences, the spiritual implications, and the theological interpretations are important but they are not a substitute for the will of God. The apostles, in the face of threats from the authorities, declared, *"Whether it's right in God's eyes to listen to you rather than to God, you decide. As for us, there's no question - we can't keep quiet about what we've seen and heard." (Acts 4:19, The Message)*

Our Lord made it perfectly clear to the disciples that obedience was expected from them. The proof of their love for him would be that they would keep his commandments. He had chosen them and appointed them so that they would "go" and "bear fruit" (John 15:12-17). We are not at liberty to refuse to preach the gospel of salvation to the whole world. We have been saved and called to live for God and to obey God as a sign that we are children of God. We are commanded to declare the gospel of Jesus Christ. Failure to do this is disobedience, not to any church authority, but to Jesus Christ himself. For this reason, evangelism and mission must come at the top of our agenda at diocesan level, archdeaconry level, in the parish, the local church, and in our individual lives. Failure to participate in mission and evangelism is to be opposed to God, for God does not desire the death of a sinner; he does not wish the world to be condemned (Ezekiel 18:23, 33:11). Therefore he has saved us and called us and sent us to warn the world to turn to God through Jesus Christ. Whoever refuses to participate in evangelism is not only disobedient, but is actually guilty of wishing the world to be condemned.

When on the ninth day of February, 1992, I was consecrated and enthroned by the Church of Nigeria as the third Bishop of Jos, I knew nothing about being a bishop; I had simply been a pastor and missionary in the Diocese of Kaduna. Having spent much of my childhood in Jos, I had come to Kaduna in 1978 for interview for the ministry, when I was twenty-two years old and had no qualification to present except my conversion story. I was accepted and sent for training at the Theological College of Northern Nigeria. After ordination, I was sent straight back to Kaduna Diocese. Later, on becoming a bishop, I was appointed to Jos, my childhood city. The Diocese of Jos had been in crisis and in canonical courts over various issues involving finance, ecclesiastical appointments etc. Consequently, the mission of the church, and evangelism, the task of the church, had become casualties!

Any diocese or church will always have an expectation about their shepherd, and sometimes their expectations would require him to be nothing short of a magician. The people are not impressed with qualifications; they simply want their problems solved, their church to grow and all their expectations to be met. In my first weeks in Jos, I read expectations on the faces of the people, and they made comments that told me a whole lot, as they said what the diocese could not do, and insisted on the impossibility of doing evangelism especially because, they said, "there is no money." Of course, they also mentioned the lack of personnel, of land on which to build a bishop's house and so on. This was enough to crush my spirit, but my faith and will were intact. The only thing I knew that I could do was to recall my conversion experience, and to recall my call to ministry and mission in the context of some days in personal private prayer and retreat. While praying I saw a picture of the direction of the mission to be accomplished; I shared this with a colleague who put my vision into a small, illustrated write-up now known as the *Blue Booklet*. The focus in the vision is the wholehearted pursuit of the primary mission and commission of the church: reaching out to children with education, training the workers, engaging in healthcare to communities, working with the people for hygiene, for clean and safe environments, together with agriculture.

Three things also came out of my retreat: first was the story of Nehemiah, and so I then travelled and went throughout the entire diocese (then covering Plateau and Nassarawa States), every village, every town, city and hamlet, praying and asking God for the salvation of the people. The second thing was the experience of my conversion and discipleship and I became convinced that beyond church planting and church expansion, the real need was to preach the gospel to people to the point of true conversion and discipleship until they became true followers of Christ. The third thing was the development of structures, which are to follow and serve the needs of the mission as will be required as the mission progresses. After some months of thinking, planning and discussions, we began with training in evangelism with a practical session of five days in a town. The result gave birth to many things, many people came to Christ, many people offered themselves to serve in the mission field and new congregations were born!

Always God is the missioner: the mission is his. We are the carriers or vehicles of that mission. When God calls, we answer; what God says, we do; wherever he sends us, we are to go. This is obedience and this is mission: the two are inextricably linked. Jesus himself was the supreme example of such obedience and of such mission. He came to announce the Kingdom of God; he taught about the Kingdom of God; he lived a life in which the Kingdom of God broke through into this world and could be seen by those who had eyes to see.

This is the example for us to copy. A living church must be a Mission Church reaching out to others who are not related by ties of blood, and going to people in need of all that will restore their dignity and humanity through Jesus Christ. We who have received the benefits of mission must now go out to give. This means not just personal evangelism in the ways in which mission has traditionally been understood, but also being socially active in community development and community transformation. This is because a true presentation of the gospel of salvation always comes with practical implications and clear evidence of the message: it is a wholistic living out and pouring forth of the love of God to all peoples, nations, tribes and communities of his world. The missionary Bishop and scholar Lesslie Newbigin reminds us this way:

> One can tell the story of missionaries who have set out with the firm determination to do nothing except preach the gospel, to be pure evangelists uninvolved in all the business of "social service." But the logic of the gospel has always been too strong for them. A hungry man comes asking for food; shall he be refused in the name of the gospel? A sick child is brought for help. There are children all around with no opportunity for school. And so the missionary has been drawn, in spite of pure

theology, into the work of education, healing, social service, "agricultural missions" and a host of similar activities.[1]

Such is the full reality of God's mission, as exemplified in Jesus' self-understanding of his own mission:

> He unrolled the scroll and found the place where it was written, "The Spirit of the Lord is upon me, because he has anointed me to proclaim good news to the poor. He has sent me to proclaim liberty to the captives and recovering of sight to the blind, to set at liberty those who are oppressed, to proclaim the year of the Lord's favour." And he rolled up the scroll and gave it back to the attendant and sat down. And the eyes of all in the synagogue were fixed on him. And he began to say to them, "Today this Scripture has been fulfilled in your hearing."
>
> —Luke 4:17-21, ESV

We must never forget, indeed, we must always remember, that as Christians, we have a call and it is a single all-important call equal to none other. Moreover, this call has eternal consequences. We will do well as individual Christians to answer this call and follow the example of Jesus. It is challenging, but we will succeed. Consider this story: When a journalist asked a missionary about his work in Africa and why he thought he could make a difference, he replied, 'We can't lose because we're putting our shoulder to a door that God Almighty has already opened.'[2] And that's the truth. This is God's idea first. This is God's agenda, and he will lead, guide, and help us as we go.

---

[1] Newbigin, Lesslie, *The Open Secret: An Introduction to the Theology of Mission*, Grand Rapids: Eerdmans, rev. ed 1995, p. 86.

[2] Pilavachi, Mike, *When Necessary Use Words: Changing Lives Through Justice and Evangelism*, Minneapolis: Bethany House Publishers, 2006, p. 108.

Digging Deeper:

1. It has been said, "The church exists to fulfil Jesus's last command." Do you agree with this statement, or do you think there are other reasons for the church's existence today?

2. Why should missionaries be concerned with community transformation?

3. Why is it important that our words and preaching are in line with our actions and practice?

4. In what ways can the church today show "compassion"? Is this being done?

CHAPTER 3

SENT OUT

I once received through the post a somewhat dirty envelope. Inside was a Christmas card (this was in August), and when I opened the card I was even more confused as some of the signatures were from people who had died! I looked again at the envelope and realised that it had arrived at its destination some seven years after it had been sent! Before any such journey can begin there must be a "sending," but being sent does not guarantee that the correct path will always be followed.

Apostolic means Sent

Whether big or small, young or old, every Christian denomination and gathering seems to want to call itself apostolic. For some, this means that they teach only the Bible - or their particular interpretation of it. For others, it means that they are orthodox in the sense that they adhere to the apostolic faith as put forth historically in the creeds. For others, it means that their bishops have a particular historical lineage that is known as apostolic succession. There are also groups that hold to some mix of all three interpretations. Tragically, many churches have forgotten that the word apostle comes from the Greek verb *apostellein*, meaning, "to send out." To be apostolic is to be sent. It may have to do with the succession of hands and of doctrine, but it has also to do with the continuation of mission and evangelism. As Robert Scudieri says:

> When we call the church apostolic, we are talking about more than just our pedigree; we are declaring the church's missionary task. Of course apostolic means that the church continues to believe the doctrine of the first apostles. But it means something more. It means that the church continues to do what the apostles did, because the church has also been sent by the same Sender.[1]

And the theologian Carl Braaten decisively states:

> Apostolicity means doing the apostolic thing, namely, continuing the cause of Jesus . . There is no other way to retain continuity with the apostles than to keep doing what they did - going with the gospel, making disciples of all nations, baptizing them in the name of the Father and of the Son, and of the Holy Spirit. That is really all that mission means.[2]

In the last chapter, we saw how the disciples learned from Jesus. In time, and empowered by the Holy Spirit, many of these disciples would become the first apostles and the first missionaries. Driven by a commitment to mission and the love of God, they converted an empire within three hundred years. Following the apostles, the early bishops too were missionaries, not bureaucrats. In *The History of the Expansion of Christianity*, Kenneth Scott Latourette writes, "When the office of bishop arose, one of the functions seems to have been winning pagans to the faith."[3] Missionary bishops such as St. Patrick and Samuel Ajayi

---

[1]Scudieri, Robert J., *The Apostolic Church: One, Holy, Catholic, and Missionary*, Chino, CA: Lutheran Society for Missiology, 1995, p. 3.

[2]Braaten, Carl E., *The Apostolic Imperative*, Minneapolis: Augsburg Press, 1985, p. 55.

[3]Latourette, Kenneth Scott, *The First Five Centuries*, vol. 1 of A History of the Expansion of Christianity, New York: Harper and Bros., 1937, p. 116.

Crowther are later examples of bishops who understood the call to wholistic mission and evangelism.

When Samuel Ajayi Crowther, an ex-slave, began his work in his own native land of Nigeria in 1842, the British colonialists had not yet come, but King Massaba, the Emir of Bida, recognised Crowther as a national leader. Indeed, his talks with the Emirs of Kano and Sokoto showed that he was an accepted national leader. This was not because he was a Bishop; it was because he placed high stakes on his people, paid the price of the sacrifice that demanded his service, his time, his integrity and all it takes to build a people. His approach was simple: to preach what he believed; to live what he preached and believed; and to teach the people, by example, what he believed, preached and experienced from God. He then transformed communities and brought peace to warring communities, introduced agriculture, fought local slave trading, built institutions of learning, health and worship in various communities; opened up inter-tribal communication, marriages and trading. All this made it easy for the colonialists when they arrived. Crowther was the true father of Nigeria. He brought education, medicine and agriculture from Yorubaland to Igboland and to the northern parts of Nigeria. He spoke Yoruba, Igbo, Hausa and English and toured virtually all the riverine local communities.

Scudieri again writes:

It was not the bishops only, but the whole church, bishops, presbyters, deacons and laity, which was authorized to proclaim God's virtues. The mission is not some disembodied will; it has been given flesh and blood in the women and men baptized into Christ. This flesh and blood is brought to life, animated, by the Spirit. Walter Freytag aptly calls the congregation "the point of breakthrough for the Holy Ghost in the world".[4]

The church historian Stephen Neill confirms this truth. Speaking of the early church, he says:

> What is clear is that every Christian was a witness. Where there were Christians, there would be a living, burning faith, and before long an expanding Christian community. . .That was the greatest glory of the Church in those days. The Church was the body of Christ, indwelt by his Spirit; and what Christ has begun to do, that the Church would continue to do, through all the days and to the uttermost parts of the earth until his unpredictable but certain coming again.[5]

Writing about Anglicanism in Uganda, Archbishop Henry Orombi said:

> Another notable effect of the East African Revival on Anglican identity in Uganda is a renewed passion for mission and evangelism. . . . .
>
> In short, an apostolic church is a missionary church. A bishop is the focus for the mission of the Church, following in the footsteps of Jesus, who commissioned his apostles to preach, to teach, and to heal. The bishop's apostolic ministry starts with evangelism, because transformation begins with the individual. The bishop himself must have a testimony and set a direction in his diocese for evangelism and church planting. When the early missionaries came in the late 1800s, their understanding of mission was not only preaching but also education and health ministry. So, combined with our churches, there are schools and health clinics, all under the

---

[4]Scudieri, p. 78.

[5]Neill, Stephen, *A History of Christian Missions*, London: Pelican Books, 1964, pp. 22-3.

apostolic oversight of the bishop, whose charge is to preach (evangelism), to teach (schools), and to heal (health clinics).[6]

The baton has been passed on. Apostolic means sent. To be called to follow Jesus is not only to be saved, but to be sent so that others may be saved. Examples of those who responded to this call will be found in the Epilogue (pages 63-67). Today, however, it is our turn to take up the task – NOW!

Considering the Cost

We tend all too easily to think that because Jesus was Son of God as well as Son of Man, everything was easy for him. We forget Gethsemane and the piercing insight that that gives us concerning the cost that Jesus had to pay - even before the crucifixion. The struggle was devastating, before he was at last able to cry "Your will, not mine, be done."

If it was not easy for the Master, it will not be easy for the disciples. From the apostles' time to the present day, many missionaries have become martyrs, and many more have suffered for the sake of the gospel. The demand and the price are high. However, obedience is the key to mission, and we must obey, even though it may involve going to hazardous places, to difficult places and to oppressed situations. Indeed this is inevitable because those people, situations and places which are outside the gospel cannot know the fullness of peace, justice and compassion until they hear and receive the gospel. No wonder that some denominations, some dioceses, some churches and some individuals will do everything to remove evangelism from the agenda of the church. In such cases, if evangelism is on the agenda at all, it is there just to satisfy the Bishop or whoever is responsible for evangelism, but it will only be discussed as a subject and allowed to

---

[6]Orombi, Henry Luke, *What Is Anglicanism?*, 2007, http://www.firstthings.com/article/2007/08/001-what-is-anglicanism. DOA 1/12/2017

fizzle out, to be discussed again later; and so long as it is being discussed, it remains purely a subject for discussion.

Availability and willingness are key factors in the task of mission and evangelism. Too often, the present day approach to mission tends to look for what the mission field can provide, or the missionary looks out for what he can get out of the mission field. Jesus, however, as we have seen, looked at the crowd and "he had compassion on them, because they were harassed and helpless, like sheep without a shepherd." (Mt.9:36). He saw the need of the people, and his interest was how to solve their problem. This is the heart of mission, for without compassion mission is impossible. It is compassion that moves the heart to act without feeling superior. There is no selfish thought of "getting," but only of self-less "giving."

We must accept that in doing evangelism we will bear the cost. It needs a lot of time in prayer, in preparation, in careful planning and training of individuals and of the church. It also takes a lot of effort to mobilize the people: it demands the total mobilization of the church, not of just a few individuals, because the command is to the church. Leaders must be "fished out," taught and trained. Christ did not issue a general appeal for disciples; he called them one by one "You . . . follow me" (cf. Mt 4:19). He then spent time patiently teaching them, living with them, praying with them. Our theological training today must be of a high quality, and it must also be geared for mission. Pure intellectualism is of no use: there must be training for service. We are to teach those who will then go and teach others, who in turn will teach others, who will teach others . . . In that way, the word is constantly handed on, each time involving an ever-increasing number of people. As Paul wrote to Timothy: "what you have heard from me in the presence of many witnesses entrust to faithful men who will be able to teach others also" (2 Timothy 2:2). This takes time; it takes energy; it needs resources; it must be rooted in prayer; it calls for a total dedication and commitment of one's life. Some people are tempted to despair and to say that the task is beyond our present capability: if we had hundreds more ordained clergy, then we could begin! Remember that when Jesus Christ began his ministry, and indeed even at Pentecost, his "diocese" was the whole world, and his "staff" twelve men, one of whom betrayed him.

Why do we not go?

The sad thing is that, whether or not it is done as a delaying tactic, some have made mission so complicated: you need money; you need transport; you need tracts, loudspeaker systems, films, band, crusade ground, security . . . and all this must be in place before you can begin! That is not what Jesus said! Jesus simply called individuals to be with him and then he sent them out. They were the people who were there on the spot; they were not outsiders who were imported to do a specialist job, which, by implication, no local person was able to do. They were there and they were available. When Jesus had first called them they had left their jobs and their market and had followed him - with no conditions attached. They had been with Jesus and learned from him, and so they could begin to share his vision. They could begin to see something of what Jesus saw. He said to them that the harvest was plentiful, although the labourers were few - and they were able to see and to do the work that lay ahead of them. Whatever it was that he now wanted them to do, whether it was a small job or a huge task, and wherever he wanted to send them, far or near, they were willing and available, despite his warning that it was as if he were sending lambs into the middle of a pack of wolves. They were willing to take the risk, and to face whatever might come their way.

The early missionaries to Nigeria left us many examples of such commitment: they were prepared to do anything, to follow God's leading, whatever that might mean. Their vision of mission was not static, they were themselves prepared to change and adapt and if necessary to retrain to acquire necessary skills. For example, the first dentist at Vom Christian Hospital was a printer, and the first doctor there was someone who came without medical skills but saw the need and went back to train as a doctor.

Why do we not go? There is also the temptation to look at what we have started and to be content. The joy that accompanies the starting of a project can be so overwhelming that the work stops completely because everyone is admiring the beginning of a laudable programme. Very subtly, other things then choke our minds and the vision is lost. The apostle Paul would give room to no such distractions (see Philippians 3:12-13). His detractors could not stop him. Enemies from within and from without could not stop him. His own personal qualifications he put aside. His health, his condition in prison, indeed his life was completely surrendered to the task of the gospel and the mission of the church of God. The goal was set before him. Never at any point would he have thought that having started, he had arrived. In fact, he recognised that it is God who started, and it is God who will finish the task. We are both indebted to God and dependent upon him. When the risen Christ commanded his disciples to go to all nations, to preach, to teach and to baptize, he also promised to be with them, always (Mt.28:20). If, however, we refuse to obey, we lose his presence with us. Christ goes ahead of us, calling us to follow, but if we sit still where we are, then we are left further and further behind, until his presence is only a dim memory. That is surely one reason why some of the older established churches are now dying. We must learn this lesson before it is too late.

Why do we not go? Sometimes the command to "Go" has not been obeyed simply because people have not heard it. If a water pipe is blocked with dirt, the water cannot flow through it. If our lives are blocked, we ourselves cannot hear God and God cannot work through us to reach others.

Hindrances to Going

Four major hindrances that cause our lives to be "blocked" in this way are:

1. *Sin.* This is the greatest enemy of progress in the life of the believer who desires to "go." God does not send us out to advertise sin; God is a holy God who has redeemed sinners and sends them to announce the message of redemption to lost sinners. Every weight of sin must be dropped if we will go forth and have a hearing (Hebrews 12:1).

2. *Worldliness.* We get caught up with worldliness and settle on "making money," building empires and concerning ourselves with what people say about us, and so on. These do not get us far because they only last for this life (Mark 8:36).

3. *Disobedience.* Some Christians have hidden under laziness to become disobedient when God is calling us today to "Go forth." Others are simply deliberately disobedient and become agents of confusion in the church.

4. *Distractions.* Distractions and diversions will keep us busy but totally ineffective. This is clear right from the time of the early church when, for example, an administrative problem brought complaints and grumbling, and threatened to cause a major division in the fellowship (see Acts 6:1-7). If the

apostles had not seen the danger and dealt with it, they would not have been able to preach and to go forth as their Master had commanded.

"Go forth" must imply "be open": nothing can "go" through a closed door: God's word cannot "go" through us if we are closed up, and if our lives are blocked in any way. It is a privilege that sinful people like us should be considered to speak on behalf of God. Let us therefore not be disobedient, but let us hear the command to "Go." Let us be sent.

Sheep and Wolves

In being sent, however, we must take heed. Our Lord warned the disciples: "Now go, and remember that I am sending you out as lambs among wolves" (Luke 10:3, NLT). The disciples are to be like lambs: they are to be harmless, gentle and completely dependent on the protection of their owner.

But, we may ask: if Christ's followers are the lambs, who or what are the wolves which threaten them today? Obviously, there is outright persecution, whether motivated by political, social or religious concerns. There is also the more personal persecution of mockery, abuse or even threats at work, at home, or in the streets. Other wolves, however, have already found a hole in the wall of the sheep-pen, and are moving closer in among the sheep. These are the more insidious and grave dangers of false teaching; of a "gospel" to which something has been added or from which something has been taken away; of the concern for status, money, and position within the church; and of an unwillingness to serve and to suffer. These wolves are far more dangerous than many people realise. The truth is that outright persecution has never killed the church; it has been said correctly that the blood of the martyrs is the seed of the church. False teaching, however, can be responsible for the death of the church in a particular location. The demise of the early church in North Africa has already been mentioned, and a major reason for this was their totally inadequate teaching and practice of mission and outreach to the local communities. Wolves can also appear in the guise of such things as economic hardship, difficult conditions, temptations not to struggle to learn a new language, and the like.

Wolves such as these have always, and will always, be prowling around, sometimes close by, sometimes further away, but always ready to attack. This was true in Old Testament times and as Jesus sent out the disciples. Jesus knew that it would continue to be true for all his followers. But he still sent them out – and they went willingly, willing to face whatever risk there might be. They obeyed Jesus, and there is a huge advantage in obeying. If you "go" in obedience to the Lord, then it is the Lord's responsibility to look after you – and he will never fail in this. If, however, you refuse to obey and refuse to "go," you can be sure that the wolves will come and seek you out wherever you are, and as you have already put yourself outside the Lord's protection, see your trouble! More even than that, however, those who refuse to "go out" to other people become not lambs, but wolves in sheep's clothing. They are the ones who will influence others wrongly, and thus lead them astray.

A final thought: it is also interesting to note that the other "sheep" to whom the disciples are sent are said to be in a sick condition and in need of healing; possessed, and in need of deliverance; depraved and in need of salvation (v.9). Does not this describe some of our churches, and indeed our fallen world!

Digging Deeper

1. Consider your own church. What priority is given to Mission? If Mission does not have a high priority, why do you think this is, and what can you do about it?

2. You are called to go out on mission as a "lamb." Who or what are the wolves you face in your own situation today? How can these wolves be faced most effectively?

3. Are you afraid of these wolves? How will you overcome this fear? Discuss and encourage one another.

CHAPTER 4

THE UNREACHED

After a mission training, the participants were sent out to talk to people on the streets. One man spoke to a person who was selling oranges directly opposite the church. That person received Christ, but then asked, "I have been selling oranges here for a very long time, but no-one has ever before come out from your building and told me about what you do in there, or spoken to me about Jesus. Why?"

Whenever "the unreached" are mentioned, people think of remote areas. We must realize, however, that while the unreached may be in remote areas there are also unreached people in our own neighbourhood, as well as amongst our immediate family and friends. Just before the Lord Jesus Christ ascended to heaven, he said, *"you will receive power when the Holy Spirit has come upon you, and you will be my witnesses in Jerusalem and in all Judea and Samaria, and to the end of the earth"* (Acts 1:8, ESV). The progression here needs to be noticed. The disciples were told to begin in Jerusalem, that is, in the city where they already were. After that they would gradually move out in ever widening circles, first to the nearer lands, Judea and Samaria, and ultimately to the ends of the earth. The starting point, however, was the home base.

Crossing Cultures

On several occasions, one of our city churches organised a major mission outreach to a rural area in a far corner of the diocese. That was in some ways a laudable project, but it raised two important issues. Why had they gone to that far place when they had not done evangelism in the area immediately surrounding their church? Moreover, even in that far place why were most of those whom they contacted successfully members of their own tribe and not indigenes of that area? It is true that there is a sense that it can be more difficult to engage in evangelism and mission within your own family, your local area or amongst your work-mates. One reason for this is that these people know you well: you cannot talk to them about Christ's call to love one another, when they constantly hear shouting and arguments from your own house! One the other hand, however, in a country like Nigeria where there are very many different tribes, there is a tendency for Christians to relate primarily, if not exclusively, with other members of their own tribe. This leads to tribal churches, who only worship in their own language and thereby exclude their immediate neighbours who come from a different tribe and language group. This is clearly contrary to New Testament teaching as shown for example in Paul's appeal to the Ephesians:

> I therefore, a prisoner for the Lord, urge you to walk in a manner worthy of the calling to which you have been called, with all humility and gentleness, with patience, bearing with one another in love, eager to maintain the unity of the Spirit in the bond of peace. There is one body and one Spirit—just as you were called to the one hope that belongs to your call— one Lord, one faith, one baptism, one God and Father of all, who is over all and through all and in all.
>
> —Eph.4:1-6

The early church struggled over the relationship between Jews and Gentiles, the circumcised and the uncircumcised, but eventually the leaders were led by God to see that Gentiles should not be expected to become Jews before they became Christians (Acts 15). All were to be one in Christ. In evangelism today, we may meet a variety of prejudices, misunderstandings, traditional aversions, even out-dated feuds and desires for revenge. We shall encounter tribal barriers, colour prejudices, racial and national fears and oppression. Differences of language, customs, unspoken communication, traditional ideas and ways of thought can all raise barriers. Such barriers were broken down on the cross of Christ, but we, as Christ's ambassadors must show in our lives as well as in our teaching his universal love and compassion. As the hymn writer puts it:

> In Christ there is no east or west,
> In him no south or north,
> But one great fellowship of love
> Throughout the whole wide earth.[1]

There is another practical advantage to evangelising your neighbours. If you evangelize only the members of your own race or tribe, or only the people you like, the result is that when Satan's demons come they will leave your church and your members alone, but they will enter your unevangelized neighbours' homes and lives. This means that you will never know peace - precisely because you have not evangelized your neighbour! Your children will marry their children and you will have an ungodly or demonic in-law. Your children and grandchildren will attend the same school as the children of the ungodly. Today we hear stories of cults and satanic activities in secondary schools such as

---

[1]Oxenham, John (1852-1941)

we have never heard before. Is not this because we have not obeyed God by doing evangelism?

When your neighbour does not hear the gospel you will not know peace, and so at prayer meetings you will pray like this: "Protect me from my neighbour." You have not visited your neighbour; you have not prayed with your neighbour, made friends, shared, or shown love. So what do you expect? In fact, if this state of affairs is allowed to continue it will not be long before the children of the ungodly begin to rule and oppress the church.

As we noticed earlier, God's mission is very clear: *"God so loved the world that he gave his only begotten Son . . . ."* (John 3:16). No one is excluded; everyone is included. The unreached, therefore, includes every person who has never heard the gospel in such a way as to respond either positively or negatively. This includes those who may have heard with their ears but not understood. Or they may be people who have a vague idea about what the Christian gospel is, but they have not been privileged to have the gospel explained to them because of their nationality or because of state restrictions. There are also the unreached who have not heard the gospel largely because of the church's inactivity in reaching out to their particular areas. Finally, there is another group of unreached people who are in the cities and are not evangelized because of the church's large assumptions that the unreached are in faraway rural places and not in the cities. These types of places exist both in Africa and throughout the world. Here are big mistakes and the church needs to be corrected.

Still we must first understand the need to evangelize the lost: it is a life-saving mission! As was discussed in earlier chapters, there can be no doubt that it is the desire of Jesus and his command to the church. The question is, however: do we truly understand the urgency of this task and do we have a desire to complete it? As Bishop J.C. Ryle once said, "We ought to feel for them as if we are true Christians; we ought to pray for them; we ought to work for them, while there is yet time. Do we really believe that Christ is the only way to heaven? Then let us live as if we believed it."[2] Again, in the words of the Strasbourg Reformer, Martin Bucer, "Therefore, since it is the Lord's will that his lost sheep should be led to his flock and his sheep-pen and become one flock, those who are to serve the Lord in seeking his lost lambs and bringing them are not to relax their service."[3]

In some parts of Nigeria today we are seeing a rapid growth in the number of churches opening, and in the number of people giving their lives to Christ. We thank God for this, and give him all the glory - but truly, we have scarcely begun! There are still thousands in this nation, and in every other nation throughout the world, who have not heard the gospel. Thousands of people are uncommitted, and many thousands of children running around our streets who do not receive any Christian teaching. The people in the towns, the traders, the homeless children, the prostitutes, the poor, the sick, the rich, the rural people: everybody must be told the good news by word and deed. They must also be discipled and taught to live lives worthy of their call. Radical change and transformation are required. This means that we must talk to the hearts of people in ways they will understand; we must set before them living examples that they can see and imitate. There must be an uncompromising presentation of the truth of God's word as it is, in love and full of the Holy Spirit. We must preach not ourselves, but Christ crucified. We must not be conformed to this world, but we must be transformed through the work of the Holy Spirit by the power

---

[2]Ryle, JC, *Knots Untied*, Moscow, Idaho: Charles Nolan Publishers, 2000, pp. 42-43.
[3]Bucer, Martin, *Concerning the True Care of Souls*, Edinburgh: Banner of Truth Trust: 2009, p. 79.

of the word of God. In this regard, we have only just started and, like St. Paul, we must press on (Phil.3:14).

Children

According to the gospel records, Jesus did not often show displeasure or anger. This means that when he was annoyed it will have been about something very significant (like the cleansing of the Temple), and the disciples will have taken serious note about it. On one occasion, recorded in Matthew 19:13-15, the crowds were following Jesus as usual. Perhaps the disciples could see that Jesus was tired and they wanted him to rest; the last thing they wanted was a crowd of noisy, boisterous children! So they tried to keep the children, the mothers and their babies away. Jesus saw what was happening and rebuked them sharply saying, *"Let the little children come to me and do not hinder them, for to such belongs the kingdom of heaven."*

We owe it to God and to the next generation to ensure that children today come to the knowledge of the gospel of the Lord Jesus Christ. Every child that is born comes to this life with a seed, and no one knows what kind of seed the baby is bearing. No one knows who the next Governor, Bishop, President, President's wife, Bishop's wife, pastor's wife, sexton or catechist is going to be. Every child must therefore be adequately cared for, given the maximum attention, presented with the gospel early enough and given the chance to receive the Lord Jesus Christ.

In Nigeria in particular, we have come this far as a church because of the sacrifice and labours of our grandparents and parents who saw education, not as a means of making money, but as an avenue of giving a future to the oppressed. Our parents and grandparents provided education in order to give freedom and the opportunity of gaining a livelihood. The mission schools here were in content and purpose theological. They taught children how to pray, taught children to have respect for humanity, for the environment and, most of all, taught children how to serve God and one another. The graduates of these schools became catechists, evangelists, clinic attendants and dispensers, teachers and assistants in various forms to the missionaries. Much later, the colonial officers came and although they were white, they were unlike the missionaries in that some of them were stark unbelievers and pagans. They required from the missionaries a manpower supply of honest, dedicated and educated local people who had received mission education. These were to be clerks, storekeepers and account clerks in the treasury. Such people were readily at hand and were faithful in the discharge of their duties - so much so that the colonial officers always continued to look up to the mission for the supply of manpower. In other words, theological education became useful to both the church and the community. This was true throughout Plateau and later on in the government of Northern Nigeria. These standards must be restored and developed. We must restore the quality, content and theology of raising potential leaders from the grass roots of our educational systems.

We must go back to the original vision for education in our schools. Here in Jos Diocese we will provide education in the schools and in the church using our Prayer Book, catechism and the Bible. We will provide education for prayer and praise of God, and give an opportunity for education of all ages, right from nursery to adult. This ministry is not something to be kept in the background; it should be at the forefront of our agenda in every church.

Churches must give priority to Sunday Schools. If the Sunday School is merely a place for keeping the children out of the way of the main service, or a time given entirely to clapping hands and singing choruses, then a huge opportunity has been thrown away and the future of the church put at risk. Sunday School teachers and those responsible for children should be trained and adequate provision be made for good materials and schemes of work. For example in Jos Diocese we have a Director of Children's Ministry, who has gathered a team of experienced teachers with various specialist skills. This team are responsible for training all who wish to teach in our Sunday Schools. Alternatively, other national or regional bodies also train those who work with children: we need to take advantage of the courses they offer.

In the same vein, every mission team should include those who are particularly detailed and ready to gather the children. In that way the children will not be a noisy nuisance on the edge of every conversation or congregation: they will be an integral part of the evangelism and no opportunity will have been lost.

Youth

It is said that 40% of the population of Nigeria is made up of youth. While in many other nations of the world the majority of the population is over 50 years of age, in Nigeria, the majority of the population is below 35 years of age. One of the greatest hopes for this country lies in this teeming, active, young population. Statistics put the youth in Nigeria at between 60 and 70 million. This means that for a long time to come there will be a growing generation. Such a generation needs to be guided, nurtured, trained and established on a firm foundation for the building of the nation. This puts us in an advantageous position, and the only problem is whether we see only the downside, the violence, the destruction and the suffering in which our youth may be involved, or whether we see the opportunities in the future lives of our youth. The church must find ways of reaching out to our youth with the gospel of Jesus Christ. Hence, we must have young, committed pastors and youth workers: these can relate with their own generation much better than adults who are ten, twenty or more years older.

This is an urgent task because the youth are the foundation of our society. Their energy, inventiveness, character and orientation define the pace of development and the security of a nation. Through their creative talents and labour power, a nation makes giant strides in economic development and socio-political attainments. On their dreams and hopes, a nation founds her motivations; on their energies, she builds her vitality and purpose. It is also because of their dreams and aspirations that the future of the nation is assured.

There is, therefore, an urgent need to involve our youth in decision making at appropriate levels; develop for them a comprehensive programme of education and socialisation, and make them good and productive citizens. We must also provide them with opportunities for vocational training geared towards self-employment and self-reliance, as well as the spirit of adventure, resourcefulness, inventiveness and the virtues of patriotism, discipline, selfless service, honesty and integrity. It is hoped that this will inculcate in them a sense of discipline geared towards making them socially responsible and accountable.

The youths are a volatile and vulnerable group with peculiar needs and aspirations. The majority of our youths face problems that include inadequate parental care, non-availability of suitable sports and recreational facilities, moral decadence in the society, lack of appropriate role models, religious fanaticism, cult activities, political manipulation of youth organisations, unemployment and under-employment, poor education, breakdown of family values and indiscipline.

The range, extent and magnitude of the problems that confront the youth today require a committed and determined effort on the part of the Church in order to help them to achieve their potential. These problems need to be addressed urgently and should be an essential part of our mission outreach. It is pertinent to note that so many of the youth are very intelligent and highly endowed, but they need avenues, opportunities and encouragement to put their talents into use. Young committed Christians must be encouraged, trained and commissioned specifically to reach out to the youth. Moreover, this should be done with the positive, prayerful, financial, understanding support of the rest of the church.

Adults

Similarly, adults today are going through all the varied realities of the hard road that is this journey we call life. Some have had a broken start, some are feeling weak, some are unfulfilled, some are successful, and some are tired of trying: the list of adult situations is endless and varied. It is the ability of the minster or evangelist to walk through these experiences with the people in their struggles, successes, and failures - all the while making the gospel relevant and thus able to transform their lives and situations - that will make the flock, in turn, become missioners in the larger society. The number of disciples was increasing in Acts 5: and this was without any major event, except that they kept speaking of their testimonies on a one-on-one basis to friends, relatives, and neighbours. We should also notice that the Christians in Acts did not allow lack of resources amongst the new believers to be an issue. Rather, they cared and provided for widows, the needy, orphans and the poor. They were open to all tribes, races and all conditions of people, who often had their necessary needs met because the young Church had developed a workable and accountable system built on selfless trust, totally devoid of selfish pride, of sectarian display, of capitalist division between rich and poor in the family of Christ!

Urged on by St. Paul (1 Cor.16:1-3, 2 Cor.9:6-7), the young believers were always encouraged to "give" rather than to concentrate on "getting"! Sadly, many congregations today seem not to have learned this crucial lesson. Some of those around us may have particular needs, including widows, orphans, the sick, the elderly and the poor, those in prison or in hospital. To ignore these is to contradict the gospel! In the gospel, we see how Jesus addressed the needs of the people in addition to preaching the message. The gospel-in-action is simply how a converted Christian lives: it is love-in-action. Assess the needs, meet them, and you win a hearing.

My wife and I have found this to be true with the vulnerable children we have worked with at the Zambiri outreach, both with the fifty children who live with us, and with the more than 400 who come to our school where they receive free education, free meals, and free medical care. Vulnerable no more, they are simply our children, with no partiality or distinction. We love them, and God does the rest. God's provision for all their needs is simply amazing. We cannot change them, or the trauma and experiences of their short, hard lives. However, the care and love we give them is often a vehicle for the love of God to enter their hearts, and then the gospel can change them. We can testify to this. Moreover, the adults who have joined with us in this enterprise have themselves found joy and fulfilment, knowing that this is indeed the Lord's work.

Whether the unreached are in our own yard or on the other side of the world; whether they speak our own language or have a completely different culture, tongue and tradition; whether young or old; these are the "lost" for whose sakes our Lord Jesus Christ came into the world

(Luke 19:10). These are the very people whom Christ came to "seek." These are the ones to whom we are to go now.

People of Other Faiths

God created the heavens, the earth, and all the people in it. This means that God created people of all faiths and practices. Still today, some have not had the chance to hear the gospel, some have heard but turned away, and some do not even care. We, however, have heard the gospel and have committed ourselves to follow Christ. One of the many implications of this is that we must live together with all other brothers and sisters whom God has created, whether or not they believe in Him. As we recognise the fact that many do not believe in Jesus Christ, or hold to only a nominal or partial faith in him, so we must, in obedience to Christ, try to bring them to know, love and serve the One whom we are privileged to know as Lord and Master, Saviour and Redeemer. The power of the gospel of the Lord Jesus Christ must be seen in our lives so that, even if we say nothing in words, peoples of other faiths will be challenged by our lives, and surprised by our perseverance.

To bear witness to the love of Christ with people of other faiths is therefore not primarily a matter of academic debate, of round table discussion or even of media bombardment. It is simply living the gospel of Christ in the power of the Holy Spirit, day in and day out, in such a way that others see, are challenged, and are surprised.

I was born in Northern Nigeria, and I have always known Muslims since my birth. Indeed, in happier times, we spent much time in each others' homes and were participants at one another's family celebrations and sufferings. From this I have learned, first and foremost, that whatever divides us, people of other faiths are human beings created in the image of God and thus worthy both of our love and of hearing the gospel message. In this age of pain and terror, many of us will need to spend ample time reflecting and praying on this point before we can effectively witness in a divided community.

In the area covered by our diocese, there are many Muslims as well as Christians. The evangelization of a Muslim is not a one-day affair, and we must remember that the cost is high for such a person to become a Christian. We need to ask whether our lifestyle reflects the love of Christ and his righteousness? Muslims are disciplined and serious in their faith life: do they see that in us, or do they see contradictions between the message we proclaim and the lives we live? Further, do they see in us the love, joy, purity and freedom in Christ that is so lacking in their own belief? The question is, will we reach out to them?

Digging Deeper

1. Jesus said, "For the Son of Man came to seek and to save the lost" (Luke 19:10). Why does your local church exist? What is its purpose and vision?

2. What priority does your church give to (a) children; (b) youth; (c) other faiths? How can this be improved?

3. Approximately what percentage of your local church congregation is youth? Why do you think this is? Are you satisfied with this?

PART II

WHAT ?

THE CONTENT

CHAPTER 5

THE GOSPEL

> For I am not ashamed of the gospel; it is the power of God for salvation to everyone who has faith, to the Jew first and also to the Greek. For in it the righteousness of God is revealed through faith for faith; as it is written, 'The one who is righteous will live by faith'.
>
> —Romans 1:16-17

Two-year old Salome skipped along happily, each hand held firmly by one of her sisters. Their parents were close-by, talking excitedly with their friends and neighbours. They had heard that Jesus was in the next village and they were walking there in order to see and hear him again. They enjoyed listening to him. When he talked he made things so clear that they could understand. His teaching was always interesting, not like the sermons of the official religious leaders. Their friends were also bringing their son Joshua, hoping desperately that Jesus would heal his badly broken leg. There was something different about this Jesus: it was as if the love that he talked about simply flowed out of him. Everyone wanted to come close to him.

Transformation

That same love and that same transforming power still characterise the gospel today. The Christian gospel is not about command over space or territory or even command over peoples. It is not about numbers, or numbers in politics, or gaining control over nations. Some theologians who are more interested in politics have made it look as if the Christian gospel is competing with Islam for such power and control. That is not the primary aim of the gospel! The Christian gospel is about the abundant life that God gives to everyone who opens their heart to the Lord Jesus Christ. It is about God at work transforming lives and communities, and bringing abundance of life from heaven to humanity. It is about bringing health, healing, restoration of humanity, restoration of the environment, and the restoration of the fallen nature of man and so of everything around him. It is about bringing joy, peace, reconciliation and the abundance of life that only God can give. This total transformation of individual lives and of communities can be seen from New Testament times up to today.

It is often thought that the gospel begins and ends with the preaching of Scripture in a particular style. But the gospel which Paul describes as "the power of God unto salvation" (Rom.1:16) is marked by the evidence of three key signs amongst many. Wherever the gospel has been truly preached and received, there has been evidence of an outflowing of love in action in the lives of both the preacher and the recipients, as a mark of the activity of the gospel in lives and in the environment. Secondly, wherever the gospel is preached, truth is declared, established and enthroned to the extent that lies are rejected, evil is exposed and lives are transformed. The third evidence of the gospel is the evidence of righteousness: the righteousness of God is lived out to make right things in society that formerly were wrong. People who previously could not do right, now through the power of the gospel exhibit a changed life and show forth the righteousness of God at all times and in all ways.

We can see all of this in the Acts of the Apostles, which gives us a remarkable picture of the life and growth of the young church. The joy and excitement that characterised the crowds who followed Jesus were still there. Peter's first sermon on the Day of Pentecost left the apostles with a discipleship class of 3,000! Such a movement, however, was bound to attract opposition, and one of the fiercest opponents of the young church was a Pharisee named Saul. This remarkable man was at first not just a non-Christian, but also a fanatical, militant activist, committed to the extermination of Christians and to the total eradication of their faith. After his encounter with Christ on the Damascus road, however, he was totally changed and his whole life was thereafter given not to eradicating, but to proclaiming the gospel. He became eager to preach to as many people as he could reach, including the Romans, the colonial overlords who were despised and hated by many of his people. This was, for Paul, as it is for many today, a task needing courage. Paul, however, emphasises that he is not ashamed of the gospel; rather, it is this gospel which has the power to change lives, and even to change prevailing circumstances.

In Romans 1:16-17 (quoted above) Paul encapsulates the central core of his theology and of his way of life. Paul speaks from personal experience: he knows how a person of another faith can be totally changed and transformed. The gospel is power: the original Greek word for this power was dunamis, from which we get the English word dynamite. The gospel is a powerful explosion, and has the ability to changes lives – totally!

This power is the power of God working towards the salvation of everyone who believes. It is more than just preaching, more than just talking: it is not merely an announcement of the fact that salvation will take place one day. The gospel is itself a divine power leading to salvation; it leads to faith and action, to the restoration of lives, of communities, of the environment. This is so because it is Christ we proclaim: Christ who was born, lived, suffered, died and rose again for our salvation; Christ who is now glorified in heaven and who will come again as Lord and judge. This Christ has reconciled us to God by his death on the cross; through him our sins are forgiven and we are saved from the fear of Satan and from the powers of death and hell. If we are united with Christ we become a new creation, continually being so transformed by the power of the Holy Spirit that we grow more and more like him who is our Lord, our Saviour, our Master and our All (2 Cor.5:17-21).

The salvation thus offered is available for all, of whatever tribe, race, nation or faith. Those who accept it are brought into a right relationship with God, and seek to uphold God's standards, God's way of living, and God's righteousness in the world. This righteousness produces holiness, truth and justice. Such righteousness, however, cannot be attained by keeping the law, but only by faith.

The Anglican tradition summaries the gospel in Article 11 of the 39 Articles:

> *XI. Of the Justification of Man*
> We are accounted righteous before God, only for the merit of our Lord and Saviour Jesus Christ by Faith, and not for our own works or deservings: Wherefore, that we are justified by Faith only is a most wholesome Doctrine, and very full of comfort, as more largely is expressed in the Homily of Justification.[1]

This was the battle cry of the Reformation: the recovery of our freedom in Christ. In Romans 5:1-11, Paul explains it this way:

---

[1] Article 11, "The Articles of Religion," in *The Book of Common Prayer*, The Church of Nigeria (Anglican Communion), CSS, Lagos, reprinted 2002, p 863

> Therefore, since we have been justified by faith, we have peace with God through our Lord Jesus Christ. Through him we have also obtained access by faith into this grace in which we stand, and we rejoice in hope of the glory of God. Not only that, but we rejoice in our sufferings, knowing that suffering produces endurance, and endurance produces character, and character produces hope, and hope does not put us to shame, because God's love has been poured into our hearts through the Holy Spirit who has been given to us. For while we were still weak, at the right time Christ died for the ungodly. For one will scarcely die for a righteous person - though perhaps for a good person one would dare even to die - but God shows his love for us in that while we were still sinners, Christ died for us. Since, therefore, we have now been justified by his blood, much more shall we be saved by him from the wrath of God. For if while we were enemies we were reconciled to God by the death of his Son, much more, now that we are reconciled, shall we be saved by his life. More than that, we also rejoice in God through our Lord Jesus Christ, through whom we have now received reconciliation. (ESV)

The bad news is that before we are saved, we are dead in our sin. But, "while we were still weak, at the right time Christ died for the ungodly." His sinless life and atoning death provided freedom from sin and eternal life - while we were still sinners. Like the prodigal son, all we have to do is to come to our senses, to wake up, and to return to our Father's house. That is the good news! This is why evangelism should be such a joyful task! Unfortunately, because the message is so simple, throughout the centuries people have attempted to add to it, to make it more acceptable to unbelieving human ears. The church went through the Reformation in order to recover this truth, and must always be undergoing a process of reformation to stay close to this essential truth of the gospel of Christ.

In considering what this gospel is, we need to take note of three vital factors:

The Gospel for the Whole World

Jesus had begun his ministry by quoting from the prophet Isaiah (61:1-2):

> The Spirit of the Lord is upon me,
> because he has anointed me
> to proclaim good news to the poor.
> He has sent me to proclaim liberty to the captives
> and recovering of sight to the blind,
> to set at liberty those who are oppressed,
> to proclaim the year of the Lord's favour.

The concern here is for the poor, the broken-hearted, the blind, the weak and the vulnerable. The ones whom the established religion did not want to know, were the very ones who were on the top of Jesus' agenda. He came to seek and to bring into the Kingdom the least, the last and the lost.

Therefore, at the foot of the cross there is no favouritism. Living for Christ is living for others, for all others. It is service delivery; it is missionary; it is a total dedication and commitment to Christ and to obeying him. If as Christians we desire to bring others to Christ, to establish the reign of truth and righteousness in society and finally attain everlasting life, then the only way to live is to surrender to Christ, to die to self and live to serve others. This kind of life will spark revival in the family, bring transformation in the community, and renewal wherever such a servant of Jesus Christ is found. The missionaries of old are great examples of this. No matter what the opposition, no matter how fearsome the juju looked, no matter how entrenched the tradition, no matter what the cost might be, they continued undeterred, living and teaching in such a way that people of all faiths or none might see the transforming effect of the gospel. The gospel was lived before the eyes of the entire world, young and old, rich and poor, men and women, people of any and every race and tongue, tribe and nation. The gospel is for all and we must dare to reach out to all (as was discussed in chapter 4 above).

The Power of the Gospel

The gospel is powerful, as is demonstrated by the death and resurrection of Jesus Christ. By that single event, we see the final defeat of Satan and of all the powers of hell, of sin, of death and of evil. It is therefore, no use at any point in life or time, submitting or surrendering to the devil because Jesus Christ has defeated the devil and all his powers.

It is not possible for anyone to come in contact with this kind of saving power of the gospel and with this kind of experience and remain the same. This kind of experience with the power of the gospel will always produce a radical fire-brand believer whose main aim is to serve and please God, bringing life, light, peace and joy wherever he goes. The explosive fruit of life is the evidence of the reaction of a person who has met with the power of the gospel. This is also true where a family, church, or community has come in contact with the gospel.

Therefore, anyone who receives and believes the gospel must speak the truth at all times, to all people, and must do so in love. To live in truth is also to insist on standing for justice for the oppressed and on giving justice to all people regardless of their race, religion, nationality or gender. It is significant that it is the gospel's power that manifests God's righteousness in us and empowers us to live righteous lives in such a manner that even unbelievers will acknowledge that believers of the gospel are practising righteousness. Those who do not believe the gospel understand very well when they see people practise righteousness and live in holiness.

To live in this way, however, requires three qualities:

a. It takes a determined, cumulative *effort* to keep teaching the word of God until the truth of how to live and obey God's word is learned, accepted and obeyed. We are to be channels through which the power of God can work, and such channels must not become blocked by laziness, selfishness, unfaithfulness or any other kind of sin.

b. Secondly, the gospel must be lived out with undiminished *consistency* in service to God, to the community and to all people. We must show people by example in small and in big things, everywhere and every time, what it means to carry and to live out the gospel.

c. Thirdly, we must be *diligent,* faithfully seeking to live as Christians who truly believe the gospel. We must bring our faith to bear in all that we do, in order to bring glory to God in everything, and to bring blessings to the people around us.

Here is the privilege and here is the cost of living in the power of the gospel.

The Eternal Effect of the Gospel

The gospel calls for a decision that each person must make and such a decision will determine the eternal destination of that person. Such a decision, when made, must bring the believer's life into conformity with the eternal truths of God, of his Son Jesus Christ, and of the Holy Spirit. God's word is truth, and every one of his righteous ordinances endures forever (Psalm 119:160). Therefore, the gospel must go beyond mere verbal assent! It starts with a verbal confession and acceptance of the spoken message, because the gospel must be communicated and so must be responded to and consented to by word of mouth. It does not and should not end there, however, but must be so taught from Scriptures through the manner of life of the loving, caring person discipling the new convert, that the disciple is totally convinced mentally that the gospel is true.

The responsibility of moving from accepting the gospel mentally remains the next task of the teacher, and it is here that a lot of Scripture is committed to memory through careful, deliberate and consistent meetings to review faith-building Bible verses. The portions of Scripture in review must be practical and related to building faith as well as how to live the new life in a way that the believer can measure daily progress in life in community. This is the crux of the daily test of a growing life of a Christian: the commitment to take full responsibility to live out the faith according to Scripture is tested daily and with each success of practicing Scripture comes increase of faith. The step to firm up everything that has been taught, read and confessed is the long journey from the head to the heart. The gospel must travel beyond verbal assent, beyond mental assent: it must reach the heart in all its fullness and must get down with its full content and power to shine out in the transformed life of the believer. The power of this gospel will and shall produce a powerfully transformed life, bearing fruit of transformation with a remarkable life of repentance, an active life of service and a genuine sacrificial living for the benefit of others. This kind of gospel life becomes a transformed transformer anywhere – just as was the case with Saul who became Paul.

When persons, communities or churches truly respond to the gospel there is a new joy, a new freedom, a new eagerness and zeal. The more a person makes up his or her mind to do the will of the

Lord zealously, the more they will find that doing God's will brings joy, peace and contentment. In fact, boldness grows as pleasure in doing the will of God increases. Zeal is a necessary ingredient in action whenever anyone in the service of the Lord is going to please the Lord. It is the drive for mission, the key to ministry and the engine of all victory over impossibilities, fear of failure and all postponements. Lack of zeal is lack of drive and the absence of the sense for urgency. When a man or woman is in the service of the Lord and lacks zeal, the devil is comfortable because such a person will settle to excuses, procrastinations and blaming other people. However, when a person is zealous for the Lord, obstacles become a battle, excuses become an enemy, complaints become idolatrous and procrastinations become chaff until such a person, consumed by zeal for the will of God, accomplishes the task. Zeal is the propeller that brings joy in accomplishing the will of the Lord! It unlocks the door of God's promises and covenant for anyone who is determined to be zealous for the Lord! As a result, the following characteristics tend to develop:

1. The mission of the gospel becomes priority, evangelism takes place quite easily, and evangelism is a mark of each member of the family. The daily concern is of reaching the unreached, serving the poor, the needy, orphans, widows and the forgotten. The high and rich are not neglected while the gospel is not restricted.

2. There is a natural recruitment programme for children, youth, and students at all levels, working class, artisans, politicians and all other groups. The natural power of the gospel works smoothly amongst the fellowship with only one aim: always to make new disciples of Christ.

3. Intercession is a major mark of such a group or fellowship or even family. Intercession is not specialized to a particular group or for professionals alone. Where the gospel with its power is at work, intercession becomes a natural part of the life of each believer whose heart is given to the gospel of the kingdom.

4. Teaching is a major evidence of the power of the gospel at work. Where this gospel takes root servants and teachers are not scarce; there are servants and teachers of children, youth and adults and in all fields of mission.

5. It is not yet the true gospel until a community of faith rooted in the Scriptures, revolutionary in discipleship, transformed in character and enthusiastic in missions, evangelism and social action is established.

To bear witness to the gospel in this way means dying to self and living for Christ. To live in this way is rewarding both here on earth and also eternally in heaven, whereas refusing to die to self has no reward on earth and no reward in heaven.

Those who carry the message of the gospel will not always be welcomed; there may be intimidation, humiliation and suffering. St. Paul knew all of these, but he refused to give up. He searched out people of all faiths: Jews, worshippers of pagan idols, and those who served an "unknown god." Always, under all circumstances, his concern, his aim, his reason for living was to "press on" with this gospel (Philippians 3:12), the gospel which had so caught and transformed him, that he knew that no one was beyond its power.

This power has been given into our hands and into our hearts today. To bear witness to the love of Christ is simply living the gospel of Christ in the power of the Holy Spirit, day in and day out, in such a way that others see, are challenged, and are surprised.

A famous example of such a life in recent years is that of Mother Theresa who lived and worked with the lepers, the destitute and the dying in the slums of Calcutta in India. Her very presence brought peace, hope and light into the darkness, the dirt and the destitution. Her work became known worldwide and it is said that on one occasion a media team came to film her work. The light inside the Home for the Dying was so dim that the camera operator thought it would not be possible to catch anything on film. However, they decided to go ahead and try it. When they arrived back at the studio and looked at what they had filmed, they were astonished. That section of film which had been shot in the gloom was the best of all: the whole place was bathed in a beautiful soft light!

Digging Deeper

1.   What does the gospel mean for YOU?

2.   Can you give any examples you have witnessed of the power of the gospel at work in the lives of individuals, churches or communities?

3.   In living out the gospel, effort, consistency and diligence are needed. What do you find most difficult here and how can we help one another?

FALSE ALTERNATIVES

I want to know Christ and experience the mighty power that raised him from the dead.

—Phil.3:10, NLT

In many countries today, television threatens to replace church attendance in the lives of many people. It is less demanding to sit comfortably at home, perhaps enjoying a meal at the same time, or relaxing in a reclining chair. Visitors may even come in and out, bringing distractions and diverting what little attention was being given to the programme. Priority is no longer given to the word of God; it now becomes a background noise, an unnoticed presence like the wallpaper. This downgrading of the power and the importance of worship, preaching and teaching has a number of unfortunate repercussions which in turn lead to false presentations of the gospel, false teaching and a totally false witness in the life-style of many so-called "television evangelists."

In saying this, it is recognised that if it is done in the right way the transmitting of services and other Christian programmes can be a great blessing to those who are housebound and physically unable to get to church. Similarly, some preachers and singers are genuinely committed to the Lord and seeking to fulfil their calling. At the other end of the spectrum, however, are those who use this medium to raise fame and money for themselves, who already own several cars and mansions and who are seeking to lift high their own name rather than the cross of Christ.

The Centrality of Christ

This is in stark contrast to the vision and focus of St. Paul who declared to the Philippian church, *"My one desire is to know Christ and the power of his resurrection"* (Phil 3:10 RNEB). Paul's focus was clear. All his preaching, all his working, his travelling, his writing, even his suffering had this one aim in view. Therefore, whenever he presented the gospel he sought not to draw attention to himself, but to point people to Christ. This was the pattern of preaching in the early church right from the time of Peter's first sermon on the Day of Pentecost. This must also be our pattern and our focus. There is no room for a competing goal of making money, or success, or prosperity, or of speculative and corrupt theologies. Indeed, any business, learning, or contribution, which does not further this one task of making Christ known and leading people to heaven, has no value other than that which is temporal and ephemeral. The apostle Paul had only one task, one goal, and nothing could come between him and this one task. He presses on; his focus is right and he strains towards the prize. His commitment was total.

True and effective evangelism cannot be done just as a token gesture. If it is attempted simply because it has been commanded, it will be done as a dry, impersonal routine, with no inspired activity, no enthusiasm and no joy. It will even be done grudgingly, as if the whole undertaking were a boring waste of time. And indeed, it will be a waste of time! Similarly, evangelism cannot even be done effectively if the only reason for its being attempted is in order to please or placate the leadership of the church, or so that you will not be accused of being out of step with the mission movement of the church.

As a church leader, I have seen too many examples of the above kinds of so-called "evangelism." Their contributions to the work of the Kingdom have actually been negative, rendering a complete disservice to mission, and setting back the work of the gospel. Because the work has been done grudgingly it can bear no fruit; after all, who will want to join in an activity which is presented as being a burden, a joyless imperative and a bore! The lack of fruit will be blamed on a lack of materials or equipment, on the weather, on the nature of the mission field, or on any other factor or person.

There are also those who do evangelism with a misplaced pride: they think they are doing a favour to the people they are trying to evangelise. They go to the mission field thinking that they are superior, and are going to do something wonderful for the poor, uneducated and inadequate people they are visiting. They may be well equipped with finance, instruments, films, and their own education, but they are totally lacking in the love and compassion of Jesus Christ. Evangelism and mission cannot be done in these ways!

Similarly, evangelism and mission must not be seen as a means of extending or enlarging our own nationality, race, family, culture or even civilisation. Those who see it in this perspective generally seek to impose their own brand of the Christian faith, culture and way of life on others for whom it may not be appropriate. This has been shown to be ineffective and unproductive because it is foreign and "un-indigenised," and therefore can put down no roots in the lives of the local peoples, and quickly dies when persecution comes.

Today we face many situations and challenges that have the potential to bring problems and a loss of vision. Heretical teachings are peddled by a variety of so-called evangelists, who are more concerned with making money and gaining a name for themselves, than they are with proclaiming the truth of the gospel. Authentic teaching and a living presentation of the true gospel in the lives of Christians, and especially of Christian leaders must counter this practice. We must distinguish the true message from the false if our evangelism and our preaching are to have any power.

Therefore, if in this day and age we are to preach the apostolic faith, the true faith, we must be aware of and reject the false teachings that are currently assaulting the gospel. In order that our preaching may be pure and our evangelism effective, let us notice some of the false teachings which are most prevalent today.

The False Teaching of Salvation By Works

In the final chapter of Reformation Anglicanism the editors, Ashley Null and John Yates III wrote:

> Every Sunday, in countless Anglican churches around the globe, the minister enters the pulpit and nags the congregation to do better for God. Progressive preachers will want their congregations to try harder at protecting the environment, fighting racism, and working toward economic equality. Conservative preachers will want their congregations to work harder at being godly, including taking practical steps to draw closer to God and serving their neighbours. Of course, all of these themes are explicitly commended in Scripture. Yet, according to the Reformers, these preachers are putting the cart before the horse. They emphasize what we should do to please God, not what God has promised to be pleased to do for us. Telling people what they should do does not empower them to do it.[1]

---

[1] Null, Ashley & John W. Yates III, *Reformation Anglicanism,* Wheaton, Crossway 2017, p191

It is true that we desire holiness in our new converts. We long to see changed lives. However, as good as this desire is, we must not let it distort the gospel of Grace. Good deeds cannot put away our sins. Only the atoning death of Jesus Christ can do this. Certainly, we do want everyone to grow in his or her Christian life. When, however, we use fear to try and motivate sanctification and growth in holiness, when we angrily say "You must do this, or you will not make heaven!" then we are undermining the very truth of the gospel that our Reformation and missionary fathers died for. We seek to add something to the cross of Christ, and we say that the blood of Jesus is too weak to save. The words of the old hymn are true: "What can wash away my sin? Nothing but the blood of Jesus!"[2] The 39 Articles put it this way:

> *XII. Of Good Works*
> Albeit that Good Works, which are the fruits of Faith, and
> follow after Justification, cannot put away our sins, and endure
> the severity of God's Judgement; yet are they pleasing and
> acceptable to God in Christ, and do spring out necessarily of a
> true and lively Faith; insomuch that by them a lively Faith may
> be as evidently known as a tree discerned by the fruit.[3]

Growth in Christ is essential. However, what we often view as an issue of discipleship is in fact an issue of salvation. We may yell, shout, and manipulate in an attempt to get Christians to behave as Christians, but have we ever considered that the real issue may be that they have not truly received Jesus as Lord and Saviour? We waste so much time trying to force the ungodly and uncommitted to act as disciples, when in fact we need to preach Jesus again and again until they are truly converted. Growth in Christ comes only from surrendered hearts, not

---

[2]Lowry, Robert (1876)
[3]Article 12, *Book of Common Prayer*, p. 435.

from any amount of fear or anger. Dr. Ashley Null says that the first reformed Archbishop of Canterbury, Thomas Cranmer, believed that:

> With reason and will both captive to the concupiscence of the flesh, only the intervention of an outside force, the Holy Spirit, could give humanity a new set of Godly affections . . . confidence in God's gracious goodwill reoriented the affections of the justified, calming their turbulent hearts and enabling in them a grateful love in return. This new Spirit-inspired love for God enabled believers to serve God 'gladly and willingly.'[4]

Discipleship and commitment will come only when we are sure that we are dealing with committed Christians, who know this love of God towards them and act out of love, not fear. Until then, no amount of pressure will have any effect on them, and in fact our insistence on certain works will undermine the gospel of Jesus in the hearts of our hearers. Nothing can be added to the saving blood of Jesus, not even Christian works. We "make heaven" only through his blood and not through anything we do or offer.

The False Teaching of Lawlessness

The previous section may sound strange to those who have relied on the power of coercion rather than on the power of the love of Jesus to transform lives. It may sound so strange, in fact, that we can be accused of saying sin does not matter and holiness of life is unimportant. Far from it! St. Paul wrote:

> What shall we say then? Are we to continue in sin that grace may abound? By no means! How can we who died to sin still live in it? Do you not know that all of us who have been baptized into Christ Jesus were baptized into his death? We

---

[4]Null, Ashley, *Thomas Cranmer's Doctrine of Repentance*, Oxford: Oxford University Press, 2000, pp. 100-101.

> were buried therefore with him by baptism into death, in order
> that, just as Christ was raised from the dead by the glory of the
> Father, we too might walk in newness of life.
>
> —Rom 6:1-4, ESV

The question is not whether holiness of life and good works matter; the question is when and where do they come from? Article 12, which was quoted above, states that they "are the fruits of Faith, and follow after Justification," and further that "by them a lively Faith may be as evidently known as a tree discerned by the fruit." What this means is this: once someone has truly received Christ, has true faith in Him, then good works and holiness of life will naturally and necessarily follow. If the seed planted in our hearts was the atoning death of Jesus for our sins, then as we grow in Christ, the fruit we will produce will be godliness and righteousness, not sin. If we truly love a person, we want to please him. If we truly give our lives and our hearts to Christ it follows that we shall want to please him and live in the way he teaches.

It is important to remember this, because of the false teaching of lawlessness that exists today. We are living in an age where anything goes, and where we are pressured by the culture to stay silent on matters of holiness, sin, and righteous living. In response, many churches have begun to teach a lie. "Christ loves everyone," they say. "He does not condemn and neither should we. Besides, all those moral teachings in the Bible are out of date. Just try and be a good person and everything will be Ok. Do what you wish." This false teaching is straight from the pit of hell. Christ did not die to leave people trapped in sin and darkness, but to deliver them from it! As Paul has said, "How can we who died to sin still live in it?" If we have truly been saved, if we are truly Christian, then we shall rise with Christ above our fallen sinful natures, whether in our homes, our families, churches or communities. Otherwise, we have emptied the gospel of its power to transform, and we will not be able to stand against all the forces that seek to tear down and destroy. Many of the churches of the West, churches that once were great and sent missionaries to Africa, have now virtually died and faded away because of this particular false teaching. If we truly love Christ, and if our evangelism and mission are to have any impact, we must not follow this false way.

This false path leads to a denial of Biblical principles and Biblical teaching as, for example, in the current arguments about homosexuality, same sex "marriage" and related gender issues. Non-scriptural ways of living all too easily become accepted as the norm – even by those who call themselves Christians. Many now accept sex outside marriage, and pornography is becoming rampant. Once one step has been taken on the slippery slope away from Biblical standards of preaching, teaching and living, the speed of the decline increases rapidly.

The only way to combat this increasing "law-less-ness" is a consistent teaching and preaching of the Biblical truth.

The False Teaching of Prosperity

The world would want us to believe that wealth, power and status have the pre-eminence. Unfortunately, some preachers and churches have been captured by the world's vision and message. Under the guise of so-called 'prosperity teaching,' such religious leaders collect for themselves power and become wolves instead of shepherds. Most of the time, they are the only ones who prosper! They cause much distress and hardship in an already difficult and strenuous situation, thereby making the people suffer and feel the effect of the bad situation twice over. For Paul, and indeed for every believer, it should be known and be made known, that power belongs to God, and therefore, for those who believe in Jesus Christ, to live is Christ and to die is gain (Phil.

1:21). This is a crucial fact and a comfort for the realization of our joy in the gospel. To tell suffering Christians that they suffer because of a "lack of faith," or that God is more concerned with material prosperity than with our spiritual state, is to bind people to the consumerism of the age and to separate them from the love of Christ. Too often people are told that if they join such-and such a church they will move up to the next level, or that we will not know any more hardship or sickness during the year. "Me I no go suffer" is a heretical chorus! What room does prosperity teaching have for the crucifixion, for a Saviour who "has nowhere to lay his head" (Mt 8:20)? In a world of "Divine Increase" and "Breakthrough," what are we to make of the martyrs? In James 1:2-4, we read, *"Count it all joy, my brothers, when you meet trials of various kinds, for you know that the testing of your faith produces steadfastness. And let steadfastness have its full effect, that you may be perfect and complete, lacking in nothing."* (ESV)

That we meet trials, or as some translations say, sufferings, is a fact of life. What is important is that we consider them joy because of the character they will produce in us as children of God. The "lacking in nothing" that James refers to is a spiritual completeness, not material wealth. To say otherwise is a lie, and to preach simple answers focussed on wealth, inevitably enriches the pastors and impoverishes the flock! Let our heart and treasure be in heaven alone, not in the things of this world.

The False Teaching of Entertainment

We often say that the ministry or a pastor is successful if large crowds are drawn. But what is drawing them? The commercialization of the Christian gospel has increased in our generation. Many have taken the world's system of entertainment into the church and have made a mockery of the cross of Christ. For them, Christ must be an entertainer, and Christianity must present itself in a way which will make them feel good, in order for them to be satisfied. The first side effect of this is, of course, that they are unable to stand in the face of hardship. They know only a momentary happiness instead of true joy. Worse than that, their faith, if it is faith at all, is temporal and emotional. The joy that Christ gives is more than entertainment; it is not temporal; it is not controlled by circumstances and situations: it is real.

In his book, *The Great Giveaway*, author and pastor, David Fitch explains the current situation well. He writes:

> We just do not think in terms of defining good worship by the way it forms people into good Christians. Instead, we look to the level of the worshipper's emotional involvement as a sign we have worshipped God well. So when we plan our worship, we end up pursuing the arousal of emotions and the "worship experience," as an end in itself, which inevitability turns narcissistic.[5]

and later he states:

> Much like a rock concert, the worship leaders encourage self-expression. . . In this way the worship resembles a pep-rally aimed at fostering good feelings of intimacy with God.[6]

While our worship should be lively, it must focus on Christ, not on the needs of the congregation or on the ability of the lead singer to wind people up emotionally. Preaching should be interesting and relevant, not dull and abstract; yet we can focus too much on preaching "to the crowd," rather than expounding the truth we have received. The

---

[5]Fitch, David E., *The Great Giveaway: Reclaiming the Mission of the Church from Big Business, Parachurch Organizations, Psychotherapy, Consumer Capitalism, and Other Modern Maladies*, Grand Rapids: Baker Books, 2005, p. 96.
[6]Fitch, p. 101.

style and content of the sermon should not be focused on ensuring the popularity or fame of the preacher! Consider the words of 2 Timothy:

> For the time is coming when people will not endure sound teaching, but having itching ears they will accumulate for themselves teachers to suit their own passions, and will turn away from listening to the truth and wander off into myths. As for you, always be sober-minded, endure suffering, do the work of an evangelist, fulfil your ministry.
>
> —2 Timothy 4:3-5, ESV

We can surely say that this time has arrived! The media-driven, entertainment culture has come into the church at nearly all levels. It may fill the pews and the offering bags, but what is important is not just the numbers in the pews, but whether those numbers are being taught the truth and discipled to grow in Christ. And so our call is what it has always been: to do the work of an evangelist and fulfil our ministry. While our services need to be captivating and relevant, what entertainment or diversion is more captivating and relevant than the true liberation found in the gospel of Jesus Christ?

The Antidote: Preach and Live the Message in Humility

In the days of the early church, just as today, false teachers and false doctrines threatened to destroy the faith of young Christians. Having outlined some of the false teachings which threaten the church of today, we need to consider how we can make sure that such falsehoods do not prevail. It was to prevent such a disaster that Paul and his colleagues prayed, worked, wrote and preached with all their might, seeking to bring people to repentance, to true faith and to new life in Christ. *"Him [Christ] we proclaim, warning everyone and teaching everyone with all wisdom, that we may present everyone mature in Christ."* (Col.1:28, ESV)

The message that Paul preached and taught in words was the message which he lived out in his daily life: there was a continuity between belief and action, and the action was urgent! A church that regards the gospel, even the true gospel, simply as a perfectly packaged parcel of belief to be handed on from generation to generation will not survive. Christ completed his work on the cross, but the effect of that has to be worked out in the lives of individuals and communities for as long as this world endures. The gospel is not an object that we can pick up, put down or hand on at will. For faith to be real, it must be lived. The gospel must so totally enter into the heart, mind and life of the believer that he or she is completely taken over by it. The root meaning of the word 'baptize' is to be totally immersed or soaked. Those who are baptized are to be totally 'soaked' in the gospel, with no area of life, no matter how small, omitted. When this happens, the life of the believer is transformed, and this has a contagious effect. Other people see the difference, and begin to ask questions. They need to see this difference, however, in the lives of all pastors and all believers. Too often, they do not. We cannot effectively proclaim what we ourselves do not practise.

"Gospel" means literally "good news." The salvation of all who come to Christ is a joy, the happiest news that there is! This means that when we approach others with the gospel our attitude should be that of Christ. There can be no room for superiority, for condemnation, or for self-righteousness. We cannot be lax, but we must be loving. We cannot give in to false teaching of works, or of prosperity, or of the gospel as mere entertainment. God's word must be presented uncompromisingly in love, through the power of the Holy Spirit working in our words, our desires, our actions and our character. Then it is that "He must increase but we must decrease" (cf John 3:30): who and what we are does not matter. We are only the vessels: the focus is on Christ. We are only the messengers: what is important is the message.

> Channels only, blessed Master,
> But with all thy wondrous power
> Flowing through us, Thou canst use us,
> Every day and every hour.[7]

Digging Deeper

1. Read Acts 8:9-13 and Acts 13:6-12. What do you learn from these passages about false teachers?

2. Have you heard any examples of false teaching? What was wrong?

3. What do you understand by John the Baptist's words: "He must increase but I must decrease" (John 3:30)? What does this say about pride and humility? Which of these characteristics (pride or humility) do false teachers generally exhibit?

---

[7]Maxwell, Mary E.

PART III

HOW ?

THE METHOD

CHAPTER 7

THE NEED FOR PRAYER

"The man who mobilizes the Christian church to pray will make the greatest contribution to world evangelism in history."
—Andrew Murray

Through prayer, lives are changed and situations are transformed. Through prayer, our relationship with God is built and grows. This means that prayer is a dialogue: we talk to God and we listen to God. Any conversation with a friend will not be satisfactory if one person only does all the talking! We must listen to what God is telling us. Prayer is far more than shouting our complaints or our endless requests to God. We must learn to listen to what God wants to say to us! After all, we may be part of the problem we are complaining about, or we may be part of the solution to this, or to another person's problem or prayer. As Mother Theresa said, "Prayer is not about asking. Prayer is putting oneself in the hands of God, at his disposition, and listening to his voice in the depth of our hearts."

Prayer is not limited to our "Quiet times" or to our attendance at church services: prayer, like any good and true relationship, is for life. We need to be alert and attentive at all times. This is particularly so because God may bring his answer immediately or after several weeks, or even years. That answer may come through our reading of the Bible, or through another person, or it may come as an idea which we suddenly have and are convinced about.

We have already seen that the mission is God's mission: he is the one in charge, and it is his work. This makes it doubly important that we wait for his instructions and then obey them. Only a senseless employee would insist that he knew better than the employer what was needed and how it should be done. He would soon find himself out of work!

The Bible has many examples of how God's prophets, leaders, missionaries and evangelists based their lives on prayer. We will look briefly at a few of these.

The Old Testament: Intercessors and Missionaries

Nehemiah was an exile, living and working at the Persian court. One day he received terrible news about the devastation of the city of Jerusalem. This presented him with a huge missionary challenge. He knew he should go and help repair the walls and bring "salvation" to the people, but how this should be done was far from clear, and not at all easy. Personally, he was deeply shocked by what he heard; politically he was in a delicate situation. He wept and mourned; fasted and prayed. Nehemiah was living in a godless situation: the people amongst whom he lived and worked at the court did not believe in the Lord God. Somehow, however, Nehemiah had kept the faith; he had stood firm in matters of religion, so that now, when the crisis came, he automatically turned to his only source of hope and inspiration. He prayed and cried to the Lord, probably for a period of about four months (if the dates in 1:1 and 2:1 and taken into account).

> [5]O Lord God of heaven, the great and awesome God, who
> faithfully keeps his covenant of love with those who love him

and obey his commands, [6]let your ear be attentive and your eyes open to hear the prayer your servant is praying before you day and night for your servants the people of Israel. I confess the sins we Israelites, including myself and my father's house, have committed against you. [7]We have acted very wickedly towards you. We have not obeyed the commands, decrees and laws you gave your servant Moses. [8]Remember the instruction you gave your servant Moses, saying, `If you are unfaithful, I will scatter you among the nations, [9]but if you return to me and obey my commands, then even if your exiled people are at the farthest horizon, I will gather them from there and bring them to the place I have chosen as a dwelling for my Name.' [10]They are your servants and your people, whom you redeemed by your great strength and your mighty hand. [11]O Lord, let your ear be attentive to the prayer of this your servant and to the prayer of your servants who delight in revering your name. Give your servant success today by granting him favour in the presence of this man [the Persian king].

—Nehemiah 1:5-11

Look at this prayer. Because Nehemiah is trying to see the whole situation through God's eyes, he is able to see the broad perspective rather than just one localised mission setback. First of all, Nehemiah acknowledges that God is a covenant keeping God: God will keep his promises to his people, but in return he demands faithfulness and purity of heart. The Jews, however, had not kept their part of the covenant: they had not kept the statues, laws and commandments given to them by Moses. Therefore, they should not have been surprised at the trouble that had now come upon them. They had been warned that if they were unfaithful to the Lord, they would be scattered among the nations, but if they returned to the Lord, and kept his commandments, then the Lord would gather them and bring them to his chosen place (Jerusalem).

In his prayers, Nehemiah was the heir to a tradition of successful interceding with the Lord. For example, when the Lord had been about to destroy the godless cities of Sodom and Gomorrah, Abraham had pleaded with God, begging that if fifty, forty-five, forty, thirty, twenty or at least if ten good men were to be found in the city, it should not be destroyed (Genesis 18:20-33). When the children of Israel were wandering in the wilderness, they had made a golden calf and worshipped it. The Lord was about to vent his anger on them, but Moses had pleaded with him, begging God to remember his promises to Abraham, Isaac and Jacob, and not to allow the Egyptians to think evil of them or of the Lord (Exodus 32:11-14). In the same way, Nehemiah now pleaded with the Lord on behalf of the people. Like Moses, he dared to stand between a holy God and a sinful people. Like Moses, he was more concerned for the people than for his own fate as an individual. Like Moses, he saw all too clearly that the people had indeed sinned and he confessed these sins to the Lord. Notice another very important point. Nehemiah so identified with his people that he counted himself guilty along with the Israelites, saying, *"hear the prayer of your servant that I now pray before you day and night for the people of Israel your servants, confessing the sins of the people of Israel, which we have sinned against you. Even I and my father's house have sinned"* (Neh.1:6).

Even before he received the news of this catastrophe, Nehemiah must have been a man of God, a man who studied the Scriptures regularly and prayed regularly. He knew what the Lord had done for his people in the past, and he knew the Lord enough to dare to risk hoping that the Lord would be gracious to his people yet once more. *"If my people who are called by my name humble themselves, and pray and seek my face, and turn from their wicked ways, then I will hear from heaven, and will forgive their sin and heal their land."* (2 Chron.7:14 - the Lord's reply to Solomon).

This raises many questions and challenges as we, in our turn, pray for the tasks of mission and evangelism ahead of us. Nehemiah's relationship with God, developed over the years by consistent prayer and study of the Scriptures, was such that he could turn to the Lord openly and honestly. His trust was such that he dared to put everything at risk, including (like Moses) his own life. Nehemiah's four months of praying had born fruit, and as he had struggled and prayed he had become both more willing, and also better equipped to become a part of the answer to his own prayer. It is no use praying if we are not prepared to become part of the answer to our prayer! But those whom God calls - whether to be part of the answer to their own prayer, or to do any other work - God also equips. Like Moses, Joshua, Jonah and a host of other leaders, missionaries and evangelists, Nehemiah was doubtless afraid, and wished that the job could be given to someone else. God, however, is the one who can remove fear, who provides strength and courage, and above all God is the one who says to all those whom he calls (as he said to young Joshua, through Moses): *"It is the Lord who goes before you; he will not fail you or forsake you; do not fear or be dismayed."* (Deut.31:8)

The New Testament: The Example of Jesus

As they lived with Jesus day in and day out, the disciples quickly saw that prayer was essential for Jesus: he spent long hours in prayer, not just the required minimum time. They realised that this was the key to his way of life, and that it was because of his persistence in prayer that he was able to achieve so much more than anyone else. His relationship with his Father, expressed and developed and rooted in prayer, was what gave vision, purpose and meaning to his life.

The daily demands made upon Jesus were heavy. In addition to training and teaching the disciples, there was usually a crowd of other people around him, all making demands, and expecting to receive from him, all pushing and running to get close to him. He needed time apart to pray.

> There were times when he quite definitely turned away from people. "Seeing the crowds" he escaped and "went up on the mountain" (Matt 5:1) to be apart with his disciples for some quality time together. On another occasion, when his disciples tracked him down and said, "Everyone is searching for you" (Mark 1:37), his response was to go to another town. He refused to submit to the tyranny of the urgent. He would not let the crowds or even human need dictate the priorities. He had the inner freedom to say "No". . . .it is directly after a prolonged period of solitude that Jesus is able to refuse, for in his silence he has discerned God's priorities and gained God's perspectives.[1]

It follows then that anyone who wishes to become a true disciple, to copy Jesus Christ, and to obey his call to labour in his vineyard, must base his life on prayer if he is to survive.

Jesus said, *"The harvest is plentiful, but the labourers are few; therefore pray earnestly to the Lord of the harvest to send out labourers into his harvest."* (Matthew 9:37-38, ESV). We live in an age when people are distracted: the things of this world weigh them down just as they did with Martha in the gospel story (Luke 10:41-42). Many, pursuing money or success, have forgotten that *"one thing is needful"* (Luke 10:42). Further, our young people often do not see a call to full-time ministry as either exciting or viable. Instead, they see the church as a dead institution full of committees, corruption and politics. Looking at their own prospects, they also realize that more money and success can be theirs in other fields of endeavour. Sadly, as long as people are

---

[1] Magdalene CSMV, Sister Margaret, *Jesus Man of Prayer,* Hodder & Stoughton, 1987, page 41-42

distracted and the young disenchanted, the church will continue to be weak and God's mission, the Missio Dei, will be left unfulfilled. We need, therefore, to do as Jesus commanded, and pray that God himself will raise up workers for mission and evangelism. It is his passion, and he is faithful, therefore we can expect that he will do it! This will have the effect of providing for the mission and reviving the church in the process: a church focussed on the Missio Dei seldom has time for long committees meetings and squabbles! What, however, can bury the mission is apathy, murmuring, and trivial distractions which assume disproportionate importance; what can bury the mission is a lack of wise elders, a lack of reliance upon the Holy Spirit, a lack of godly servants, and above all, a lack of prayer. We must rise up and pray!

The Lausanne Committee for World Evangelization has noted:

> Christ's teaching about prayer moves far beyond personal devotional prayer. He taught His followers to pray for God's purpose to be fulfilled and sent them to pray for others. Prayer is related strongly to Christ's teaching about the kingdom of darkness, about the nature of spiritual blindness and of how people are freed from spiritual bondage to become children of God that is foundational for the task of prayer towards evangelization. [2]

> Without prayer the mission and evangelism of the church will be burdensome, discouraging, done only out of duty and lacking in the discernment that comes from the Holy Spirit (Acts 16:6-10); we shall miss the joy of seeing people come to faith and fail to produce lasting fruit (John 15;7-8, 16). [3]

---

[2]Weldon, Glen, and Earl Robertson, *Prayer in Evangelism*, Lausanne Occasional Paper No. 42, Lausanne Committee for World Evangelization, 2004: www.lausanne.org, p. 9. (DOA 1/12/2017)

[3]Weldon and Robertson, p. 11.

The New Testament: The Early Church

A good picture of a typically frustrating missionary problem and how it was dealt with is to be found in Acts 6. The entire missionary enterprise was being held back because of squabbles over the distribution of food! *"In those days when the number of disciples was increasing, the Grecian Jews among them complained against those of the Aramaic-speaking community because their widows were being overlooked in the daily distribution of food"* (verse 1). On the one hand, the number of disciples was increasing and the church was growing; but on the other hand, the excitement of church growth was tempered by a regrettable complaint expressed in murmuring. One of the deadliest diseases to be inflicted upon a young church is murmuring. It will be recalled that it was murmuring that ruined the fellowship of the Exodus company and brought down the wrath of God upon them (Exodus 16:7). Such murmuring normally kills all good virtues softly, steadily and surely.

The complaint centred around the welfare of the widows whose cause God had promised to defend (Exodus 22:22; Deuteronomy 10:18). The two groups of widows here were of different cultural settings even though both were Jews (the Grecian Jews and the Hebraic Jews). Now, however, the differences were to become even greater. Murmuring had set in, and segregation had showed up! It often seems that like the early church we in this generation do not notice the devastating and satanic effect of murmuring and segregation on the church, and on the prejudice sometimes shown in the choice of location for the church's mission outreach. By his death, Jesus had abolished all divisions, yet here was the early church perpetuating such distinctions. More than that, however, the apostles discerned that social administration was threatening to occupy all their time and thus hindering them from their task of *"prayer and the ministry of the word"* (verse 4). In the presence of everyone, they declared that they were not at liberty to neglect their primary task. This was non-negotiable, but they made a proposal that from among the complaining group seven men be chosen to take on the responsibility of administering tables. This would leave the apostles free to pray and preach. Effective and efficient administration is necessary and must not be neglected, but prayer and preaching are vital and must be given priority.

The New Testament: St. Paul's Prayers

In his letters, we often hear St. Paul saying how he thanks God for the Christians and prays for them, as for example Philippians 1:3-11:

> I thank my God in all my remembrance of you, always in every prayer of mine for you all making my prayer with joy, because of your partnership in the gospel from the first day until now. And I am sure of this, that he who began a good work in you will bring it to completion at the day of Jesus Christ. It is right for me to feel this way about you all, because I hold you in my heart, for you are all partakers with me of grace, both in my imprisonment and in the defence and confirmation of the gospel. For God is my witness, how I yearn for you all with the affection of Christ Jesus. And it is my prayer that your love may abound more and more, with knowledge and all discernment, so that you may approve what is excellent, and so be pure and blameless for the day of Christ, filled with the fruit of righteousness that comes through Jesus Christ, to the glory and praise of God.

If we are going on mission, we need to pray for the area before we go, pray while we are there and pray after we have left. We cannot be everywhere at once but, like Paul, we can pray for all places and people. Paul rejoiced and prayed from prison: his own difficulties could not stop him or hinder his prayer! Moreover, Paul recognised that he was in a battle zone: *"For we do not wrestle against flesh and blood, but against the rulers, against the authorities, against the cosmic powers over this present darkness, against the spiritual forces of evil in the heavenly places"* (Ephesians 6:12, ESV).

Many people today are held captive by their world-view, by injustice, by other faiths, and by ungodly forces. Our first task of mission is to pray to the God whose mission this is that he will do the preparatory work of disarming these forces before we come in. Indeed, this is our first act of mission! So much intellectual effort can go into determining where we need to go for mission, yet the mission can easily crumble if we do not engage in prayer about it as well.

Paul knew that who he was as a person was far more important than what he did. His dependence was totally on Jesus through the power of the Holy Spirit. So must ours be in the task of mission and evangelism. Prayer cuts us down to the right size: in this age of religious professionals it keeps us from being too proud or bigheaded, thinking that we can accomplish a work for God; it also saves us from feeling too small and inadequate when faced with a worldwide task. Any missionary or evangelist who is not grounded in prayer faces the danger of loss of perspective in one way or another.

We live in a rationalistic age, and that spirit has affected the church as well. If it has affected the church, it will also affect our mission. We need to repent of this, for it is, I believe, the cause of much of our weakness and our failure. Only a living connection to God, renewed on a daily basis can produce an effective evangelist. Only consistent and fervent prayer for the workers and for the mission field can ensure that we do God's work, in God's way and thus obtain the results God desires.

> Not that we are sufficient in ourselves to claim anything as coming from us, but our sufficiency is from God, who has made

us sufficient to be ministers of a new covenant, not of the letter
but of the Spirit.

—2 Corinthians 3:5-6, ESV

I was with you in weakness and in fear and much trembling,
and my speech and my message were not in plausible words of
wisdom, but in demonstration of the Spirit and of power, so
that your faith might not rest in the wisdom of men but in the
power of God.

—1 Corinthians 2:3-5, ESV

Digging Deeper

1. What part does prayer play in your life? In mission and
    ministry? Why is prayer crucial?

2. Prayer is more than simply asking God for what you want.
    Do you agree? What else does prayer include?

3. "Through prayer lives are changed and situations are
    transformed." This statement was made at the beginning of
    this chapter. Do you agree? Do you know of any examples
    from life today of how people and situations have been
    changed through prayer?

CHAPTER 8

THE NEED FOR A STRATEGIC APPROACH

Now those who were scattered went about preaching the word.
—Acts 8:4, ESV

There is an old story that describes the re-entry of Jesus into heaven after his ascension. The Archangel Gabriel bowed and said, "Welcome back, my Lord. Have you completed everything?" "Yes," replied Jesus. "So you have successfully organised a church to carry on your work of teaching?" asked the Archangel. "Well," said Jesus, "I left behind eleven men to really start things moving." "Eleven men!" gasped the Archangel. "Is that all?" "That is all," replied Jesus quietly. "Those eleven men you chose," continued the Archangel anxiously, "were they men of great importance and scholarship?" "No!" said Jesus, smiling. "As a matter of fact they are very ordinary, working men." "But what if they should fail?" asked the Archangel. "The whole enterprise will have been in vain! All that suffering on the cross will have been wasted!" The reply of Jesus was firm and confident, as he said, "I have no other plans."

In many African towns, cities and even rural areas today, we hear accounts of how the number of churches has doubled, trebled, or even quadrupled. In areas where this has not happened, and in the hearts and minds of many in the mission field, this raises the obvious question,

"How?" How did this happen? What methods were used? Was there a plan, or was it that certain gifted individuals haphazardly went about preaching the word? Just as some preachers carefully prepare their sermons while some others seem to rely on "instantaneous inspiration," does evangelism and mission require careful planning, or is it all done by sudden, on-the-spot activity?

These questions demand answers, especially when we begin to appreciate how much God depends on us, and how he has entrusted this life-saving message to us! Just as Jesus, at the Ascension, left all in the hands of eleven men, so today we have been given the privilege of being the ones with the responsibility of taking the saving message of the gospel to the whole world. The numbers have increased, but the task and the responsibility remain immediate and awesome. It is such a weighty responsibility to be counted worthy of participating with God in the delivery of the good news that was, and is, the only capable, competent and potent instrument of saving the whole world. Our sense of urgency, vision and mission must take on a new speed and meaning.

The fact that the mission of the gospel of salvation had come under threat, both from within and from outside the community, prompted the apostles to develop a master plan for the evangelization of the world they knew (Acts 6-8). A brief look into the early operation of the leadership of the young church, together with a few of their Old Testament precedents, reveals some basic guidelines for church leaders of all ages, at all times in the mission venture.

Strategic Focus

The early chapters of the Acts of the Apostles give us small pictures and sharp insights into the manner of life and development of the early church. In chapters 4, 5 and 6 we hear how the devil tried to destroy the church. In Acts 4, the Jewish authorities tried to suppress the gospel of Jesus Christ by force. Because they had healed a lame man and were preaching to the people, Peter and John were arrested, imprisoned and then brought before the Jewish council, who began to question them. But, "when they [the rulers and elders] saw the boldness of Peter and John, and perceived that they were uneducated, common men, they were astonished. And they recognized that they had been with Jesus" (Acts 4:13). Public opinion was in favour of the apostles, and so the authorities decided to caution them and let them go. The apostles' response must have further infuriated them, when they boldly said, "Whether it is right in the sight of God to listen to you rather than to God, you must judge, for we cannot but speak of what we have seen and heard" (v .19-20).

Not long after this, internal corruption threatened to destroy the fellowship by hypocrisy (Acts 5:1-11). Ananias and Sapphira sold a piece of land and brought the proceeds to the apostles – pretending to bring all, but in reality keeping back a part. Their deception and lies brought instant death to both of them.

We have already seen how in Acts 6:1-7 the devil, having failed in those two earlier attempts, tried for a third time to destroy the fellowship by using the underhand tactics of distraction. God, however, always has a solution. The apostles brought in carefully chosen extra staff and through prayer and the power of the Holy Spirit, the mission surged forward.

In all these cases, the apostles refused to lose focus; their vision was clear. The apostles knew what they had been commissioned to do. They were totally committed and dedicated to their task. Their trust in God was total. Throughout the Old and New Testaments, God's leaders showed the same clarity of thought and vision. Despite any personal fears and feelings of inadequacy (as with Moses at the burning bush in Exodus 3) they put their trust in the Lord, and their confidence, clarity and leadership qualities were such that others were willing and able to follow them.

- Faced with the hostile city of Jericho, Joshua had a clear plan, told the people what to do, gained their trust and obedience – and the battle was won in an amazing way.

- Nehemiah was faced with a huge problem: the need to rebuild the walls of Jerusalem, at a time when he himself was living as an exile in a foreign land, and serving at the court of the king of that land. After months of praying and preparation, his plans crystallised so that when, at great personal risk, he asked the king for leave of absence, he was able to tell the king exactly what he needed and how he was to go about the task.

Other faithful prophets and military, religious and community leaders show similar qualities. The focus and vision must be clear if the mission is to succeed. This is so because nothing can compare in importance as a revelation for mission, ministry and evangelism given by the Lord. Nothing is as sweet and exciting in driving a passion as when a given revelation is confirmed in God's call for Mission, ministry for evangelism. No sane spirit filled person holding such revelation will follow any diversion or digress into other directions in time wasting activities. No person with such a revelation will spend time in struggles for position, power or recognition. In contrast, a person so convicted and focused on this revelation will think through the revelation, dream of how to accomplish the revelation, design a plan for action, follow through this God given revelation and soak everything and everyone in prayers. When God sees the heart of such a serious person, God will mobilize help from everywhere and direct them towards such a person.

God's mission done in God's way will never lack Gods resources. The results will show in surprising accomplishments.

If this revelation, vision and conviction are missing in the life of any mission and ministry leader then there will be activities without results, routine of religion without results, and the environment and the people will be blamed and branded as difficult, if not impossible. On the other hand a totally convinced heart given to the Lord for mission, armed with a revelation and vision from the Lord, filled with the Holy Spirit and equipped for the mission anywhere, leads to a result that is unpredictable, always glorifying to God and blessings to people! Mission is now possible!

Strategic Planning

The work of evangelism benefits from good, careful planning. This is the heart of true mission, which is biblically rooted, which takes account of legitimate grassroots movements and is sustainable.

Nehemiah had a long journey ahead of him, but he knew the route, he knew which territories he would need to cross, and so he could request letters of safe conduct, as well as for the provision of the timber he need for the work ahead of him. When he eventually arrived in Jerusalem he again spent several days preparing and silently (by night) reconnoitring and assessing the situation on ground. He could then lay a clear plan before the local leaders, so that when he called them to "Come, let us start rebuilding," their reply was immediate and equally straightforward, "Let us rise up and build" (Nehemiah 2:18-19). Such work inevitably aroused opposition, intimidation, insults, ridicule and attempts to stop the work and bring about the downfall of Nehemiah. Nehemiah's constant response was to encourage the people by reminding them of presence and power of the Lord, "Our God will fight for us!" (4:20). Ultimately the wall was completed, and the witness was seen by all: "when all our enemies heard of it, all the nations around us were afraid and fell greatly in their own esteem, for they perceived that this work had been accomplished with the help of our God" (6:16).

The situation facing the apostles in Acts 6:1-7 also required careful, godly handling. The complaint about the feeding arrangements impinged on matters of tribe and tradition, and the apostles noticed that the case at hand was capable of hampering the mission as a whole, or diluting the gospel or killing the mission. So after deep and prayerful thought, a good and workable plan was mapped out. It was a plan that seemed right to the Holy Spirit and to the whole of the young Church on how to move forward with the mission in such a way that no one would be left out. The result of this strategic planning is obvious: in Acts 6:7 we read that even priests were converted to Christ! Following that, we see the massive expansion that came out of the successful planning for the mission. At the same time, the selected seven new deacons served the widows, but they themselves never left their original calling to be missionaries for the gospel. Thus by chapter 8 of Acts, Phillip had reached Samaria, Azotus and Caesarea, including a desert outreach to a traveling pilgrim who was an Ethiopian eunuch. In fact, Phillip was later to meet the apostle Paul and his companions at Caesarea.

The apostles were spread out over a large area, with no easy communications such as are available today, and with virtually no means of transport except walking, or going by boat. Nevertheless, they maintained contact with one another and with the young churches, and when need arose representatives gathered together to address a particular situation and plan the way forward. This is clearly seen in the account of the Jerusalem Council as recorded in Acts 15. The central issue at hand was crucial: must Gentiles be circumcised and become Jews before they could be baptised and become Christians?

The whole assembly listened intently as accounts were given of what God had already done among the Gentiles. Reference was also made to the Scriptures (Amos 9:11-12), and a conclusion was reached which satisfied everyone, and gave a firm basis for forward planning and the continuing of the mission.

From these, and other examples, we can draw out the following guidelines for planning and for dealing with threats to the mission of God:

a.   Listen to all involved, listen to all the issues and pay attention to the areas of hurt, misconceptions and real or exaggerated fears. Hurt, misconceptions and fears are key: unless we address these well there is no chance that the church can unite behind mission and evangelism!

b.   Analyse carefully, prayerfully, transparently and honestly the whole of any matter that is honestly presented, taking special consideration of making a decision on a solution that must be honouring to God alone. While we must recognize that those in the body can tell lies, it remains our task to try to discern the truth as it is found in the light of Christ Jesus.

c.   Everything must be done in the light of the Word of God and for the promotion of the Kingdom of God. We must note that special explanation and attention must be given to the position of the gospel so that the message is not lost in the process.

d.   It is inevitable that internal struggles will arise in the life of a church. But they must be dealt with lovingly and not allowed to distract the leadership from the Mission of God.

Strategic Mission

In any mission enterprise, there is a need to study the environment, taking time to understand the people, their tribal, cultural and traditional worldviews, making a decisive effort to research and to gain a careful understanding of the people whom you are called to serve. The focus is on how to win the people to Jesus Christ and make them disciples of Jesus, so that they in turn may be effective missionaries and transformers of society. If our work does not produce the next generation of missionaries and transformers, or is somehow alien or foreign to the community we have been labouring in, then our mission is grossly lacking in strategy.

We need to know where we are serving and what it is the Lord desires of us in that particular place. This is important because it is the only reason why we can claim a vision for serving in a place at any given time. Those serving in the full-time ministry of the church must remember that in accepting the call to ministry, they accept to go wherever they may be sent – without complaint! If this is not so, the mission suffers and becomes self-centred and self-serving. Consider the Apostles: they gave their all and withheld nothing; they laboured diligently, faithfully and fruitfully. It was Simon Magus, not the faithful followers of Jesus, who attempted to turn the mission of God into a mission for self – with dire results (Acts 8).

There are different approaches available to the church based on the needs and the doors open for mission. These include education, health care, media, agriculture and sports. Bishop Samuel Ajayi Crowther[1] understood his call and mission, so his vision was clear. He saw that what would stop the slave trade was the introduction of trade in agricultural produce, and for this to succeed education,

---

[1] See Jesse Page, *The Black Bishop,*

both academic and practical, was a necessity. In addition, healthcare was needed for the workers. Then what followed was commerce and community development, leading to prosperity. This was a holistic mission with clear planning and strategy.

Throughout the years, one of the best avenues has been educational work. Sadly, however, many churches now look at education and schools as a means of generating money as opposed to expanding mission. Further, in some contexts, government regulations have become so intrusive and oppressive that education has practically ceased to be a viable form of mission and outreach. This is a pity, as Deuteronomy 6 calls everyone to be a teacher: in the family, on the road, in the market, on the farm and indeed everywhere. The main motive for education is this: to train children to grow in the fear and love of God, in love for neighbours, and to participate in community development and in the mission of the Lord.

We dare not miss our opportunity for missions! This is what counts in eternity, this is what matters to heaven and this is the mission of God. Having that mind which also was in Christ Jesus, we humble ourselves and become servants of all, including the dying thief, the poor widow, the Samaritans, the Jews, the Arabs, the Europeans, Africans and all the forgotten in the society. As we have seen, participation in the mission of God is so central to biblical thought that after conversion and discipling, mission and evangelism are to be our first concern. All Christians must be involved in mission, and must in turn train other new Christians to do the same. This process is what kept the apostles' ministry aflame and replicable from one community to another and from one tribe to the next. It is never the Mission of God until it becomes both replicable and repeatable in the apostolic pattern.

Strategic Method

It is important to remember that we "preach" by all that we do, say and are. People remember the sort of person we are rather than all the words we may have said. St. Francis of Assisi was a famous preacher, and there is a story that one day a young man arranged to follow him to learn how to preach. They set out. On the way, they stopped many times to help people: a child had fallen over; a woman needed help to lift her loads; some youngsters were fighting. Even when they reached the town they met someone whose mother was in hospital, so they went to visit her. By now it was getting late, and the young man was wondering when St. Francis would start preaching. At last, St. Francis said, "Now we can go home." The young man asked him, "But when are you going to start preaching?" "What do you think I've been doing all day?" replied St. Francis.

What we are is vital. We are to be like the glass in a window: we do not want to look at the glass: we want to look through the glass to see what is outside. People want to see God through us! Similarly, Scripture says that we are to be like yeast or salt: in itself it is something almost unseen, but the effect of yeast and salt "goes forth" throughout the food and completely changes its character (Luke 13:20-21; 14:34-35). We too can be used by God to help to change people and situations. There is so much need for change in the world. We talk of being "open to change," but change implies risk: we do not know exactly what will happen or how it will be. So we have to trust God; we must go forth with prayer, trust and faith. Nevertheless, go forth we must, because we must obey the command to "Go!"

We have examples of different methods of evangelism throughout the New Testament, but the key principle has always been, "what you have heard from me before many witnesses entrust to faithful men who will be able to teach others also." (2 Timothy 2:2, ESV). A careful study will show that Jesus' method was exactly this. There were at least 70 who were his disciples, and out of the 70 he selected 12 whom he called apostles. For evangelism to be effective there must be a careful selection of a workable method within each context. The principles set out above, however, always remain constant. On the whole, the small details of particular, specific methods of evangelism then become a matter of selection. Each evangelist and missioner will select the most suitable equipment, materials and particular method that will produce the best results in their sphere of influence. There may be audio recordings, videos and tracts which are very good but may not be the best in one place, while the same materials will bear fruit elsewhere.

From a lifetime of mission and ministry, the following principles have emerged:

a.   Three things to avoid:

I.   Never present the setback for mission as lack of money because it is not.

II.   Never present a request for money as the primary reason of your presentation or as the main instrument of mission or motivation for success in mission. Always remember you are not called to be a beggar nor to present a beggarly gospel.

III. Never present a pitiful picture of your work nor a pitiful condition of the people you serve. Never shame or present the shameful conditions of the people you want to serve.

b.   Motivate people to pray so that they are convicted to become involved in family, community.

c.   Mobilize people to see God at work in your work no matter how small that work is now.

d. Convince people as to why your mission is part of the great commission.

e. Convince people to know that you are a serious, accountable and transparent missionary. Introduce your family, because family is very important to the gospel and a very critical issue in evangelism. Tell your conversion to Christ, your call to mission and your ministry.

f. Be willing to present a report of your entire mission in writing with actual pictures and with an audited account.

g. The ultimate missionary credential is cross-cultural when the missionary leaves everything behind to embrace what new things God will teach through other cultures where you learn to enter into the new cultures of the people you are called to serve Phil 3:6-7. Always present Christ and insist on the Biblical gospel culture.

In the next chapter, we will briefly survey some examples of methods for mission as used in the Anglican Diocese of Jos.

Digging Deeper

1. Read again the story of Ananias and Saphira (Acts 5:1-11). What are the three main lessons you learn from this passage? How will you apply them in your life?

2. The walls of Jerusalem were broken down but none of the leaders in Jerusalem began the work of rebuilding. Nehemiah was living and working in another country, but he became the leader of this work. What particular qualities did he show which befitted him for this task, and what can we learn from him about doing God's mission?

3. What have you learned about strategic focus, strategic planning and strategic mission? How will you apply this in your church?

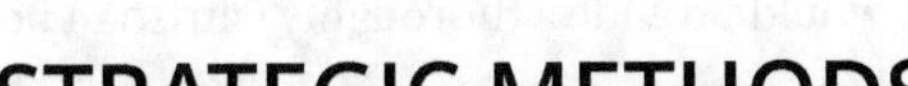

CHAPTER 9

STRATEGIC METHODS

To the glory of God, the Anglican churches in Jos Diocese have increased and grown in recent years. A brief survey of how this journey began, and what methods were used may provide helpful ideas to others who find themselves in a daunting situation.

Historical Lessons

When we first came to Jos Diocese as Bishop in 1992, we were faced with a vast geographical area and minimal human resources, to say nothing of the varied problems, difficulties and complaints that were on ground at the time. What was done and how it was done may not work anywhere else in exactly the same way, but a summary is given here as an example of what God can do if there are a core of people who refuse to give up but instead are determined to push ahead, with a clear vision and mission.

After much prayer and thought, our vision was encapsulated in *The Way Ahead* a small pamphlet that later became known as *The Blue Booklet* and in which four basic projects were outlined. We were adamant that we must be "foundation builders," and as such have an urgent responsibility to teach the children: to provide a good academic education, but also to bring them up to know Christ, and to live a

Christian life. This was necessary in order to work towards a changed manner of leadership for the future. Because of this, the first two projects concerned the establishment of two new Junior Secondary Schools, which would provide a thoroughly Christian boarding school upbringing, and would then feed senior pupils into St. John's College, Jos (an Anglican Secondary School). The schools were named as St. Mary's Convent (for girls) which was to be situated at Yerwa, and St. Benedict's Junior Seminary (for boys) at Pankshin. It was also proposed to establish a Christian Institute that would provide training for pastors, pastors' wives and leaders of the laity. A survey of the Diocese showed that there were rural areas in Plateau State where health care was sadly lacking. There were villages where anyone who had the misfortune to be sick had to trek (or be carried) over the hills to the nearest clinic. It was proposed, therefore, to start the "Gospel Medical Services," a rural health outreach scheme. Work began on these projects immediately, and they quickly became a reality.

Alongside these projects, the basic evangelism drive continued and grew. In December 1993, we had a mission in Pankshin (now an independent Diocese, but then a part of the Diocese of Jos). We went there as a team, with all the clergy of the diocese and those lay people who were interested. We spent one week in intensive training: learning how to witness person to person, learning how to pray as a team and in small groups and pairs; and learning how to develop confidence not in ourselves, but in God. Most of our sessions of learning and teaching were in the morning, while we went out for practical sessions in the evening. We also introduced another session in the last three days: we showed the Jesus film in two different locations on each one of the three days, and we intensified this with a follow-up programme every day. As for all our experiences during in that week in Pankshin, another book could be written! One thing, however, which must be noted was the joy that we experienced in seeing people receive Christ for the first time and coming for the follow-up class. Pankshin itself has not been the same since then. The churches in Pankshin have multiplied and the membership in the local church has increased; evangelism is no longer a distant theoretical statement, but something to be lived out.

In December 1994, we selected 13 people (women as well as clergy) and trained them to be trainers for mission. They received tuition from the Great Commission Movement of Nigeria, and they are also experienced in our local methods of evangelism. These people became responsible for training in evangelism throughout the diocese.

In January 1995, we declared a "Mission Week" throughout the diocese. Each parish organized a missions awareness week explaining to the members what evangelism means, what it takes to be involved in mission, who should be involved, and why there should be mission and evangelism at all. During this week there were various series of seminars, drama and music explosions. Men, women, youth and children participated in one form or another and a general awareness was created. Probably not much happened, but who is to say! Ours is to create an awareness and to mobilize the people for God to use.

Later that year we had mission placements for all the clergy whereby they spent two weeks in villages and remote areas of the diocese. A sample of the instructions given to them for that assignment is as follows:

1.   Consult the list of Missionary stations and fill in the dates. You are to spend a minimum of 2 weeks doing mission in your area of assignment. This should be completed before the end of June. Therefore, make sure that you fill in your dates for a period between January and June.

2. You are expected to evangelize; to make disciples; to start a church (if there is not one where you are going); and teach the church to be able to stand when you leave. The same church should not only feel the impact of your missionary visit, but should carry on the mission after you.

3. Do not go with your car, motor cycle or bicycle. Do not take more than your transport money (to and fro) from your local church. You are on a venture of faith and God will meet your needs according to his riches and glory.

The experience was aimed at opening the eyes of the clergy to the vastness of the unevangelized field and to the need for labourers, for prayer and for a sense of urgency in the task. This was achieved: the clergy themselves did not remain the same. New churches were founded during these two weeks. The villagers received great encouragement from the visits and God did great things. Not to be forgotten is the relationship established between the missionary clergy and these villagers, which exists up to today.

Later in 1995, each church and parish was asked to organize its own mission, appropriate for each context and carried out in its own way.

In January 1996, most of the diocesan clergy together with some of the laity went to Yerwa, Nasarawa State (now a part of the new Lafia Diocese). We spent the first day and night in prayer. We all saturated Yerwa town with a door-to-door tract campaign using the Four Spiritual Laws booklet and the Four Steps to Spiritual Growth. In the evening, we invited people to come and watch the Jesus film. The following day we divided into four groups, each group travelling to one of four cardinal locations in order to cover the whole Archdeaconry. Each of the four groups then further split into two, thus enabling us to visit 8 villages each day. This means that 24 villages heard the gospel during our three days' campaign.

In November 1996 the same pattern was repeated in the Nasarawa Eggon area, Nasarawa State (also now part of Lafia Diocese) and in January 1997 we were similarly in Langtang, albeit better equipped, better organised and with better results. (Langtang is now also a Diocese in its own right).

With each campaign, there has been a great enthusiasm and interest. We are improving and the church is being mobilized. We have seen people come to Christ in ways that only God can do. We have not spent time arguing or proving our points; we have simply shared Christ, sometimes using our little pamphlets or tracts, sometimes without them, and we have seen people come to know Jesus. The evidence of this is that such people are visibly following Christ. They are in our churches. Some are Christians who had lapsed; some were Christians only by name; some did not even know what Christianity is all about, while a good number may have Christian names, but were pagans and had never had the gospel explained to them in the way we put it. Some have wandered into our Jesus film shows and have stuck with Jesus. Some have come to listen to our music and have ended up with Jesus. God moves in mysterious ways his wonders to perform.

The other method of evangelism that we have adopted from time to time is the church planting method. In Jos, for example, in 1992 there were four churches, St. Luke's Cathedral, St. Paul's Church, St. Piran's Church and New Covenant Anglican Church. Since then we have adopted areas, spent a whole year in prayer and sought the face of God in order to reach people by the church planting method. By 2015, there were at least 47 Anglican churches in Jos metropolis and environs.

This is the Lord's work and we have to do it in obedience to his command. We must go on doing it by faith, one day at a time, looking up to him who is the author and finisher of our faith. Our experience has shown that we have made several mistakes, but the Lord has done his work. We are taking note of the following:

- In all evangelistic campaigns, materials need to be available to consolidate the faith of the new converts.

- We also learned in this venture to hold very tenaciously to the word of God.

- Prayer is participating with God, listening to God, and being available to be sent by God. Prayer is therefore the very source of the life of the believer for EVERYTHING!

- We are learning to be pilgrims, and we are learning the gift and the joy of evangelism by participating in the birth of new life in the lives of people and communities.

The concentrated campaigns are like catalysts. Evangelism is much more than these activities: the very life of Christ is seen in the life of those who believe as evidence and testimony that conversion has taken place. It is a life lived and continued in Christ, consistent with the conversion that has taken place, so that others will also be converted to Christ. This will take us through the paths of suffering, persecution, settling of quarrels, breaking down of the barriers of division, race, sex, culture, growing pains and so on. That is the life of a pilgrim - and it is pilgrims that we are called to be!

In the beginning, these outreach programmes were led by the diocesan bishop. By calling, gifting, and training, this was the logical choice. We have already seen, however, that apostolic means "sent," and therefore the church must recover the model of the missionary bishop, in the mould of people like Patrick, Columba, Crowther and even Wesley. This is what I believe with my whole heart: just as Jesus trained his team by himself and led them out on evangelism, church leaders should do the same if the world is truly to hear the gospel and believe. This method has always yielded results because where the leader leads in the mission, the followers follow spontaneously and the outcome is usually positive. However, there is a danger that outreach could become seen solely as an episcopal-led function. This is why leadership development is important.

The first stage of evangelism is to create the awareness of the message and to establish the purpose of the message. The second stage is to call the people and fully translate the message into the lives of the hearers. The third stage is to get those who have heard ready to dare to go out to reproduce the first two stages in the lives of other people and thus to enable yet more people to agree to become agents of this repetitive production. In Jos Diocese what was once done by bishop and diocese, is now done at Archdeaconry and even parish level, with clergy leaders who have been trained and grown to fill the role of leaders and organizers. The same can be said in many of the dioceses to which Jos Diocese has given birth. In spite of the very real persecution we face, the Kingdom continues to grow on the Plateau of Nigeria, and God's Mission (Missio Dei) continues.

The projects that were planted in 1992 have all grown, multiplied and developed. A revised edition of *The Way Ahead* was produced in 2006 and by 2013, a new revised edition was brought out for the "new" Jos Diocese, which, having given birth to four other diocese was now a much smaller area geographically. It should be noted that this last edition contains a clear Mission Statement and also a Vision for the Diocese. These give the necessary focus, so that whatever methods of mission and evangelism individuals and groups or churches may consider to be appropriate, the goal remains clear and unified. (These are reproduced in the Appendix)

One-to-One Evangelism

In his translation of the Bible entitled *The Message*, Eugene Peterson translates John 1:14 as follows *"The Word became flesh and blood, and moved into the neighbourhood."* (John 1:14, *The Message*). To the apostles, the call was always personal: "Follow me," and the most basic form of evangelism we have remains one person to another. Michael Green writes:

> ...personal evangelism is the most effective. The reason is simple: it is personal evangelism, the sharing of good news between two friends. That is the most natural thing in the world. It is also the most joyous. The New Testament is insistent that every Christian is a witness. Not every Christian is a preacher: maybe that is something to be thankful for. But we are all called to bear witness to the Lord who is in charge of our lives. Good news, as Leighton Ford puts it in the title of his book, is for sharing.[1]

For most of us, one-to-one evangelism is simply sharing with friends. As 1 Peter 3:15-16 says: *"And if someone asks about your Christian hope, always be ready to explain it. But do this in a gentle and respectful way."* (NLT). We may not have the gifts needed to stand on a street corner sharing with strangers, yet we must be "always ready to explain it," particularly among our friends, families, and those closest to us.

Three things are needed here:

---

[1]Green, Michael, *Evangelism Through the Local Church*, London: Hodder and Stoughton, 1991, p. 251.

- First, we must understand the importance of Jesus and the gospel in our own lives. Our sharing is more powerful and beautiful if we can talk about our own hope and the change it has made. A prisoner sharing where he has found pardon, a beggar sharing where he has found bread, the sick how they were healed: it is sharing the good news of what God has done, and the hope and life it has provided that makes the one to one message powerful.

- Secondly, we must recognize our place in the process. We do not convict, call, or save anyone. Rather, it is God who does all of this: we are merely his instruments. Again, hear Michael Green: "Our call is to be faithful stewards of the gospel which has been given into our charge. The Spirit's task is to apply it."[2] We need to be utterly dependent on God, in heart, mind, timing, and above all in prayer. If our prayer life is not good, if it is not regular, if we are not praying actively that God will call our family and those in our sphere of influence to Himself, then what exactly do we think will happen?

- Thirdly, we must recognize that each of us has different gifts: one-to-one evangelism comes easily for some people, not so easily for others. The friendly, the smiling, the joyful who have the excitement of Jesus in their heart are naturals for this work. If on the other hand, one does it only because they are "supposed to," if one is by nature more shy and reserved, then perhaps other forms of outreach and evangelism will be better suited. We are all called to participate in the work on evangelism, whatever method we may use.

---

[2]Green, p. 259.

Evangelistic Preaching

Whatever the text, whatever the topic, every sermon should be preaching about the Good News of Christ and encouraging the hearers to choose Jesus and the Way of Life. It is clear in the Bible from the sermons we have of such people as Jeremiah, Isaiah, Ezekiel and Peter that the climax of any message is a call to decision, a call to choose. Any time the pulpit is climbed, the preacher should be offering people the choice to leave sin, iniquity, and unhappiness behind, and to choose life in Jesus Christ. Let us remember that the pulpit is a place where one is called to serve others; it is a holy place, but it could be anywhere – in a boat, in the market, in the church, at home, or in any other place. We must love the pulpit, revere it, respect it and use it to teach the truth, bring out facts and give guidance and direction for the life of the preacher and for the lives of the listeners. The pulpit must be used with wisdom and sensitivity, the tempo and understanding of the hearers must be gauged, and they must never be in doubt about the preacher's love for God and dedication to his or her call. People are drawn to a sincere pulpit! The pulpit must never be a place of show, oratory or entertainment. It is holy place of meeting between God and man!

The evangelist is one who bears the message of the gospel throughout his life with the sole aim of bringing the good news of Jesus Christ to everybody. The evangelist is interested in bringing all the good benefits that the life, death and resurrection of Jesus Christ offer to all humanity. The evangelist is not satisfied with a few isolated parts of the world knowing about God, because the command of Jesus to the disciples after resurrection is to go to all the world and make sure the world becomes disciples of Jesus. It is to this world that Jesus must be Lord of all, not through force or fear but with love in action, bringing freedom from sin, oppression, degradation and dehumanization. To call one an evangelist whose view and ministry is limited to a particular tribe, race or local community, and is lacking in concern for the New Testament vision of the evangelization of the world, is an error. An evangelist of the Bible desires no less than to make sure that the world and indeed the whole world hears the gospel with sufficient understanding to be able to make an informed decision.

The evangelist brings the good tidings that bring a radical turn around in life as a whole. The message demands a verdict; it calls for conversion, a change of heart, a consideration of the message of salvation that reaches the innermost being of a person with a well-informed attention to warrant a decision for a life changing experience forever. Without this, preaching is entertainment; without this, ministry is a formal employment with a lost purpose of mission in ministry, a waste of time and of eternal resources.

The Gospel Centre Numan: a unique story

One of the remarkable things with a serious engagement in evangelism is the inevitable fact that evangelism by its very nature, when done in the power of the Holy Spirit, sparks a new dimension of unsolicited evangelistic results.

Kwalinga is in an area of Numan (Adamawa State, Nigeria) that is notorious and is well known for its twenty-four hour social activities involving alcohol, the abuse of illicit gin as well as the use of other chemicals. The Lutheran Cathedral Church is only about 200 yards away from the various social drinking parlours in Kwalinga. I was invited by the Lutheran Bishop to take a four-day Revival Meeting at the Cathedral Church, hosting not less than five thousand persons every evening. Unknown to me, loud speakers stationed outside the Cathedral were transmitting very clearly to the hearing of all in the local Kwalinga area. On the fourth morning of my stay, I was visited by twelve young men, led by a man I would call their gang leader. They came to ask for my help because they wanted to register an organisation that could provide legal assistance for their members whenever they ran into trouble with the police. As the discussions continued I shared with them my testimony of how I became a Christian, how I became a preacher of the gospel, and how God called me to serve the church. I shared with them how I no longer needed any legal help because Jesus had paid it all for me, and my life was now in his hands, for his service to all peoples in the world. The leader of the group, whom we will call Peter, asked probing questions as to how this was possible. We ended up with an informal Bible study without the Bible being in any hand, but our discussion was so free and to each one of the questions they asked I responded from Scripture with personal testimonies. One of them said, "Sir, we've been listening to your sermons since you started preaching three evenings ago, but we cannot come to the gatherings because we are not good enough." Peter, now said, "Could you, sir, please meet with us separately because the number of followers I have is nearly up to one hundred." We agreed to meet in Ward 3.

Ward 3 was the name of the second most highly respected drinking parlour, but by divine providence, it was on the land belonging to Zambiri Ngbale, my wife Gloria's late mother. Since her demise in 1979 the plot of land had been undeveloped and so the drinkers had colonised it and built a shed for customers - all without permission. While we were having our unscheduled Bible Study discussions with this group, Gloria was moved in her spirit to evacuate the drinking parlour from her mother's land. She felt the Lord convicting her of allowing her mother's land to be used for the destruction of young lives. She felt like a hypocrite, preaching and seeking the lost while doing nothing about the evil taking place on her mother's property. She therefore moved with the prayer team who had come with us from Jos to demolish the beer pots, remove all the grain for the beer, the firewood and all their utensils from the land, and she sealed the whole place.

Meanwhile, we had agreed to meet there with my group at 7a.m. in the morning so that I could talk with the larger group about Jesus. God in his infinite wisdom had moved ahead of us to prepare the hearts of the lost souls of Kwalinga and before we were born, had given the vision to Gloria's mother to purchase the land where on this day we were going to be preaching for the salvation of souls.

We met as planned at 7am in a cleansed Ward 3 with over 96 young people. Twenty-seven were baptised that morning. That gathering became what is known today in Numan as The Gospel Centre. The Gospel Centre today is a thriving congregation of over three hundred members, several of whom are in ministry, some ordained, some trained as workers in Health and Evangelism, and quite a number have regained their lives, gone to school and graduated from various tertiary institutions. The Gospel Centre Football Team is a very active platform for the youths to interact and share their faith. In collaboration with Missionary Outreach Ministry headed by Dr. Bitrus Audu, the church has visited and shared items of food and clothing to orphans and widows who were victims of the Boko Haram attacks. The Church has adopted the Mission mandate of the Diocese of Jos and is running fast with it, hence the prospecting for potential new frontiers for mission in Cham Mountain in Gombe, Riganage, Lamurde, Gyawana, Bali, Kpasham, Mauo, Belwa, Fufore, Mubi and Michika in Adamawa state and Zing, Jalingo, Kakara and Gembu in Mambila Plateau of Taraba State.

The youths have been so discipled that they are now reaching out to others like them, and this has led to the planting of three other churches apart from the Kwalinga Center, namely: Goro with 57 members, Goli with 85 members, Imburu with 65 members and

Gospel Centre Sabo with 35 members. All of these Mission outstations meet under trees, apart from Imburu who meet in a classroom. It must also be noted that six lay ministers who have been raised and groomed from the Kwalinga Station man these stations.

The story goes on, and this story is significant because I was originally invited to preach in the Lutheran Cathedral where many people came to Christ, but the result of my visit was the birth of The Gospel Centre, which also gave birth to other missionaries who are faithfully serving today around the mission field. Obedience to the Holy Spirit in evangelism gives birth to great results in missions beyond one's expectation or imagination.

Digging Deeper

1. Will this chapter change your ideas about Mission and Evangelism in any way? If so, how?

2. As a group, consider your own church and surrounding area, or the area for which you are responsible. Bear in mind factor mentioned in the chapter, and discuss what may be the most effective ways of evangelism for you.

3. Formulate a definite timetable and plan based on your decisions.

CHAPTER 10

THE NEED FOR TRAINING AND LEADERS

The final missionary step as regards the people
of any nation or culture, and the most important
lesson we will ever teach them – is to leave them.
Missionaries can never, themselves, be the end
of the line, the reason for their own existence.
A missionary in any place should never
plan for himself a missionary successor[1]

Handing on the Baton

Vincent Donovan (1924-2011) was a Roman Catholic priest, then Bishop, whose book *Christianity Rediscovered* is an account of his remarkable work amongst the Masai people of Tanzania. He was clear that for an indigenous church to survive, it must stand on its own feet, with indigenous people leading it. If this is not so, then when the missionaries finally leave, the church will die. Similarly, this is why in our own diocese we are seeking out young indigenous leaders who can be trained and encouraged to take charge of the church in their own

---

[1]Donovan, Vincent J., *Christianity Rediscovered: An Epistle from the Masai*, SCM Press, 1982, pages 163, 195

areas. If this is not done, and there is a crisis with threat to life, then the pastors and members who come from another part of the country are most likely to run back "home," and the church will flounder.

A missionary or church leader, therefore, should always be trying to train and build up the leadership capabilities of local people who will then be able to succeed him. It may well be that as the missionary hands over responsibility for one part of his work, so another door opens for a further development or a new role for him, which in due time he will also hand on. In looking for suitable people who can eventually become leaders, it will not generally be a matter of advertising and asking for applications. Jesus Christ did not ask for volunteers to be his apostles, he watched and waited and prayed, and at the right time, he simply fished out the ones whom he believed to be God's choice, saying, "You – follow me!" This is a pattern that is found repeatedly in the Bible, and it is a pattern that we shall do well to follow as we look for those to whom we shall pass on the baton.

That we must pass on the baton of church leadership to a local pastor is not a matter of choice; it is non-negotiable. The alternative is that the work dies with us. It is our responsibility to fish out future leaders, to teach them and train them - and then be ready and willing to hand over to them. It is an urgent and important matter that people from within the local community are equipped to continue the missionary's work. If this is not done, the church will lack good roots and may quickly die, particularly if the area is threatened by insecurity that causes those who are not indigenes to run away to their areas of origin.

Sadly, however, our world today is in a hurry, and too often expects the emergence of a Moses without the wilderness experience that Moses went through. As Tokunboh Adeyemo rightly said,

"Leadership without a price tag is nothing but a Hollywood fantasy."[2] There is nothing like "an emergency sanctification," a quick shower bath and suit of new clothes which can equip a person for a leadership position, whether in mission or in any other sphere.

Jesus himself, and later St. Paul, devoted a great deal of time, effort and energy to producing followers who could then become useful tools in God's hands. The leader must be a person of vision who can communicate and mobilise the people; he commands respect and trust. "Trust does not come with a stroke of activity. Trust in a leader is only built over time. . . It depends on how he maturely, tenderly and lovingly handles each little thing that pertains to men behind him."[3]

It is truly said, "like begets like": the followers will copy the leader, taking his lifestyle as their own model and standard (for example, in terms of obedience, holiness, commitment and hard work). As always, our character preaches far more volubly than do our words – and although the length of time that we preach from the pulpit may be limited, we are preaching through our character twenty-four hours a day! To quote Gbile Akanni again, "That is why God does not rush to appoint men into spiritual leadership. Men in spiritual ministry do not only preach the gospel but they must produce men after their own kind. If your life is not right, then you will contaminate the church by perpetuating your own kind."[4]

We may sometimes be able to deceive other people, but we can never deceive God. God does not look at appearances: God looks at the heart. When God told Samuel to anoint the new king, the prophet

---

[2]Akanni, Gbile, *What God Looks for in his Vessel*, Peace House Publications, Gboko, 1999, Preface
[3]Akanni p.2
[4]Akanni p.8

called Jesse and his sons to the sacrifice. Samuel looked at Eliab and was so impressed that he thought,

> "Surely the Lord's anointed is now before the LORD." But the LORD said to Samuel, "Do not look on his appearance or on the height of his stature, because I have rejected him; for the Lord does not see as mortals see; they look on the outward appearance, but the LORD looks on the heart."
>
> —1 Samuel 6:6-7

God is looking for usable people, those whose hearts are true and those whom he can trust for the future. "Sometimes God does not pick a man for his service, not because of what wrong that man has already done, but because of certain tendencies in that man's life or what the man is likely to do in the future which God has already seen."[5]

As we seek to equip future missionaries, evangelist and leaders, we are constantly challenged to look at our own lives afresh. Are we people whom God can trust? Are we truly seeking to let Christ be seen in our lives – all the time? Are we ready for anything God may ask of us, at any moment? When Samuel told Jesse to call his sons together for the sacrifice, they had to be sanctified before they could approach. David, however, came in just as he was – even while he had been tending the sheep, he had been ready for God. God is looking for usable people. Gbile Akanni has reminded us that: "Rain is good, but if there are no containers to collect it, it will waste and cause erosion. God is withholding revival, not because He does not want it but because He has not found hands that can handle it."[6]

---

[5] Akanni p.16
[6] Akanni p.7

The centrality of service in love

As we look at the character and work of missionaries, evangelist and leaders, it is important to consider the crucial notion of service. If we ourselves do not have the humility and the love to serve and also to allow others to serve us when we may truly need them to do so, then we shall not be ready to hand over the baton with integrity and love.

God through Christ chose to reconcile fallen sinners to himself out of love, and therefore we need evangelists and missionaries who are motivated by love and compassion. There is no room for anger, power, prejudice or fear-motivated preaching in this task. It has been said that "people don't care what you know, until they know that you care," and we need workers who are joyful, caring people, confident in the Good News of salvation, ready to imitate the Lord Jesus.

> Jesus, knowing that the Father had given all things into his hands, and that he had come from God and was going to God, rose from supper, laid aside his garments, and girded himself with a towel.
>
> —John 13:3-4

The disciples were horrified: how could the Master serve the disciples! It certainly was not the custom of the day. Most people would simply regard such a task as being "beneath their dignity," but Jesus lost no dignity or status by doing this. The trouble is that today an "office" tends to be cluttered up with all kinds of trappings, most of which are unnecessary, some of which are ungodly, and a few of which are downright destructive.

Gottfried Osei-Mensah comments:

> It is only as we who are called by the Lord are sure of who we are, and of our relationship with God, that we will be freed in ourselves from all kinds of insecurity to serve his people. . . Because the Lord knew who he was and knew that authority

> that was his, he was free to wash the feet of his disciples. Dignity is compatible with service among the people of God. Jesus did not cease to be the Son of God when he washed the feet of his disciples.[7]

Today not many people want to be known as servants. Before God, however, "servant" is a title of honour, because it marks that person out as standing in a long line of God's servants, the prophets and leaders of old. Moses was God's "servant" (Joshua 1:2); the prophets were God's "servants" (Jer.7:25); Isaiah spoke of the "suffering servant," and in his letter to the Philippians Paul had spoken of Jesus Christ himself as having assumed the nature of a servant or slave (Phil.2:7). Jesus Christ, the Son of God came down into a sinful, hostile world "to serve" (Matt.20:28).

Sadly, many people today are not prepared to serve one another; all want to "get" for themselves, rather than to give themselves in service. Some prefer to pursue greatness and power - and fall into the trap of arrogance, pride and self-centredness. In contrast to these, a servant has no right to his own life: he must work at all hours, whenever, wherever and however he may be required. It will not be easy; there will be suffering. Anyone who is determined to know Jesus and to follow him must be prepared to take up his cross. It has been observed that after ordination a young man today sometimes becomes less willing to serve and to do menial tasks; it seems that the recognition which the people instinctively give to a priest (of whatever faith) goes to his head; he rejoices in the status and wants to have nothing more to do with being a servant. Instead, he expects others to serve him, perhaps to buy him a car, or pay the dowry for a wife! We

---

[7]Osei-Mensah, G., *Wanted: Servant Leaders: The Challenge of Christian Leadership in Africa Today.* Theological Perspectives in Africa No.3 n.p. Africa Christian Press 1990, p. 11

are called to serve, not to be served or to take away! Let us consider what we can give to the church, the community, the people to whom we are sent and whom we are supervising. What is our contribution to the Kingdom of God?

Many of the church's problems today can be solved if only we take God's solution and follow his principles as the early church did. The problems of many churches in Nigeria are numerous and yet they are all similar: the clamour for leadership positions; the use of tribal cliques for selfish ends; glaring and outright insincerity; misappropriation of church funds; tribal sentiments and segregation. Worse still, sin is condoned under the cover of sympathy, and much church leadership is corrupt and empty. Therefore, of course, prayer cannot be said meaningfully with one accord, nor can the preaching of the gospel be done. Even if the gospel is preached it has little or no impact. The smaller, younger denominations easily sweep our membership into their churches as a result. The case was not so in the early church. They sought and found God's solutions to their problems, followed God's principles and the result was great and glorifying to God. The Word of God spread; the number of disciples increased and even some of the religious leaders accepted the faith.

Today we need leaders like Nehemiah, people of faith, prayer and integrity. We have taken each other to court; we have fought one another, and we have defrauded the offerings of the church. We have even divided the church according to tribes and instigated each group to war against the other. We have neglected the command of God to love, and we have obeyed the devil's command to destroy each other. Is this not a matter of serious concern? In fact, we in the church must forfeit every moral right to speak to our nation until we have set in order our churches and church leadership; until we demonstrate what leadership is, by following the Biblical examples. Leaders such as Moses, Joshua, Nehemiah and the apostles did not stop at concern: they prayed and took action. This is the most serious part of the whole process. Concern alone is useless if you do not offer yourself, your time and your resources for service.

We should always keep before us that picture of Jesus washing the disciples' feet, and challenging them to serve God by serving each other and all God's children. Jesus said, "I have set you an example. You are to do as I have done for you." As we try to serve we may all find ourselves struggling with our pride, our self-importance and our self-concern. We need to bear in mind Archbishop William Temple's words: "humility does not begin with the giving of service; it begins with the readiness to receive it." This is the humility we need as we become older, or when we become sick and we need others to help us. This is also the humility we need as we hand over the baton to younger leaders, leaders who may, in time, be more effective than we have been. Without a true understanding of humility and service we shall not do the work of a missionary or evangelist in the way that Christ would have us do. Our love will be marred.

A great modern hymn puts it this way:

> Brother, Sister, let me serve you,
> let me be as Christ to you;
> Pray that I may have the grace to
> let you be my servant, too.
> We are pilgrims on a journey,
> fellow trav'llers on the road;
> We are here to help each other
> walk the mile and bear the load.[8]

There is so much to be done in the church today. God is as always still searching for servants. In the same way in which Jesus spoke

---

[8]Gillard, Richard A.M., *Scripture in Song* (a division of Integrity Music Inc), 1977

concerning the harvest in Israel, "The harvest is plenty, but the labourers are few" (Matthew 9:37), so is he speaking in our time and in our context today. What our Lord is looking for is servants (labourers) - and nothing else! We need people who will bring solutions to the many problems of the church. Those who are willing to serve must have a discerning spirit and must never be distracted from preaching and living the gospel. Like Stephen and the other deacons (Acts 6:1-7) they must be people full of the Holy Spirit and wisdom. They must be ready, if necessary, to die for the gospel.

Missionaries may sometimes say that they are ready not only to talk but also to listen, not only to teach but also to learn, not only to give but also to receive. This claim, however, can only begin to be understood and to be made real, as we give our lives in love and service to Christ and through him, to one another. This is only possible if our lives are rooted in prayer and grounded upon our relationship with God. Only then will we be able to understand and to fulfil the words of a "Missionary Litany" written by a Methodist Bishop of Costa Rica:

If you cannot identify with the sufferings, anguish and
aspirations of these peoples made prematurely old by an
unequal struggle that would seem not to have end or hope:
Missionary, go home.

If your allegiance and fidelity to the nation of your
origin is stronger than your loyalty and obedience to
Jesus Christ, who has come "to put down the mighty
from their thrones and exalt those of low degree":
Missionary, go home.

If your dogmatism is such that it does not permit you to
revise your theology and ideology in the light of all the
Biblical testimony and the happenings of these times:

Missionary, go home.

If you are not able to love and respect as equals
those whom one day you came to evangelise as lost:
Missionary, go home.

If you cannot rejoice with the entrance of new peoples
and churches into a new maturity, of independence, of
responsibility, even at the price of committing errors such as
those you and your countrymen committed also in the past:
Missionary, go home.

But, if you are willing to share the risks and pains of
this hour of birth in which our peoples are living, even
denying yourself; if you begin to rejoice with them
because of the joy of feeling that the gospel is not only
the announcement and affirmation of a remote hope, but
of a hope and a liberation that is already transforming
history; if you are willing to put more of your time, of
your values, of your life at the service of these people who
are awakening; then stay, for there is much to be done,
and hands and blood are needed for such an immense
enterprise in which Christ is pioneer and protagonist.[9]

Digging Deeper

1.   Bearing in mind that Jesus Christ came "not to be served but
     to serve" why do you think it is that many Christians today
     not want to "serve"?

2.   How does the Missionary Litany (above) speak to you?

---

[9]Carden, John (ed.), *Morning, Noon and Night, Prayers and Meditations from the Third World*, CMS London, 1976, page 56

3. The hymn quoted above says: "We are here to help each other walk the mile and bear the load" (see above, page the section called "The centrality of service in love" [132]). How is this reflected in the life of the church today? How is this NOT reflected in your church? What positive steps are you going to take to rectify this?

CHAPTER 11

CONCLUSION

"In the world you will have tribulation. But take heart; I have overcome the world."

—John 16:33, ESV

Despite the ongoing attacks, bombs and threats, the church stands, and by God's grace it will continue to do so. Nevertheless, we must be fervent in prayer and totally committed to God's Mission, the Missio Dei. Remember the almost extinct North African church, or the churches of Revelation now vanished into modern Turkey. The evidence around us today points to the unwelcome fact that the message of the gospel can degenerate in just a few generations. We must stand firm therefore in our gospel message and our gospel task. The mission of the church, however, cannot, will not and will never be discontinued. We may choose to neglect it and be careless about the whole mission of God, and indeed in a given generation with a particular group of people the baton could be dropped and the mission discontinued in that place and at that time. In such a case God's mission will move elsewhere and continue. Once Christianity was North African, then it found its centre in Europe and the West. Now the centre seems to be moving to Africa: God will always find a way.

We must remember the facts: when Jesus died on the cross, he took the power of sin and dropped it in the grave, and left it there. He also left in the grave all the powers of death and hell. He came out victorious from the grave. He triumphed over all the forces, whether Satanic or human, which keep us in bondage to sin. This means that when we wilfully continue to sin, we are going back to the grave and digging out our sins, insisting that we keep them and that they are more dear to us than is the work of the Cross.

The only cure is to repent, turn round and begin to follow Jesus Christ away from the grave and death. We have to keep on following Jesus very closely and living the life God offers to all who believe. Do not lose sight of him; do not be carried away with worldly affairs; do not play around until Jesus is too far away from you. Rather, do all you can to listen to him; keep your focus sharp upon him and follow him, in your own life and in the work of mission. Otherwise, when you fall into temptation and sin, you will discover that you have turned away from Jesus and you are heading back to the grave, where death and Satan await you. Always remember the wages of sin. In spite of global inflation and all austerity measures, the wages of sin is still death (Rom.6:23). To avoid turning back to the grave, we must accept Jesus Christ and surrender our hearts totally and completely to him. To avoid others meeting a similar fate, we must be involved in this great work of the Mission of God. God's will is that not one should perish, so all must grow in grace and increase in faith, both those of us who are called Christian and those who do not yet believe. The only alternative is to return to the grave.

Christians who are not serious about their own walk with Jesus cannot successfully do mission or evangelism. When God wants them to go out, they will not. What God wants them to do, they cannot. What God wants them to achieve, they cannot. Instead, they are consumed by jealousy and hatred and are complacent in sin and lukewarm in faith. As a result, no mission takes place and the church becomes inward-focused. Budgets and programmes predominate; mission recedes. The church thus begins to shrink. Not anticipating heaven any more, both clergy and members want to get their own share right here on earth. Such "Christians" are unable to reach the unreached; in fact, they themselves need to be reached anew.

There is so much to be done in the church and world today. Just as Jesus spoke concerning the harvest in Israel, "The harvest is plenty, but the labourers are few" (Matthew 9:37), so is he speaking to us in our time and in our context. We must therefore determine and say to ourselves today, here and now, that the mission of God will continue to the third and fourth generation, and beyond, beginning from us. This means that we must fix our eyes firmly on Jesus Christ from whom, like the apostles, we will draw our example for the training and living out of mission and ministry. We ourselves must ensure that our own lives are rooted in prayer, built on solid Biblical teaching and preaching, and focused on mission, so that we become effective channels for Jesus Christ to use. In all our churches, we need to ensure that young, vibrant and committed men and women are attracted, trained and in turn become faithful servants in the mission and ministry of the church.

The unreached may be on our doorstep, in our village, or at our place of work; they may also be many miles away. In either case, the principle remains the same. First, we must receive Jesus Christ into our lives and learn to deal with ourselves, in our individual lives and in our churches. We must give mission and evangelism top priority, and we must live lives of obedience to the will of God. Secondly, we must motivate other people, but notice that this will only be possible if our own lives are transformed. Thirdly, we must go out in faith, trusting not in ourselves, but in Christ, who has set the agenda, whose command we obey, who is always with us, and whose Holy Spirit empowers us. The journey may be long; we may not know the route very well; we certainly shall not be able to see the end of the road; but Christ - and no other - is the way, and we must set out, and set out NOW! The mission of evangelism is to reach the unreached!

Our heritage comes from God, and we are made in the image of God (Genesis 1:27). The mission of the church is God's mission, and like the gospel, it never ends. That mission is ours to continue. The time is short; the work is urgent. We must not sleep. Mission and evangelism cannot be left until tomorrow. The time is

NOW !!!

CHAPTER 12

EPILOGUE

"THY KINGDOM COME" - from A SERMON PREACHED AT ACNA 2014

Introduction

We pray daily "Thy Kingdom Come . . ." This is not just a vague dream, a hope for some distant fairy tale land of ideal happiness. The words "Thy Kingdom come" are followed by the words "Thy will be done - on earth as it is in heaven." To pray for the coming of God's Kingdom is to pray for a powerful transformation that is active, living and present. According to Mark, Jesus began his ministry with the call, "The time is fulfilled, and the Kingdom of God has come near; repent and believe the gospel" (Mark 1:15). Therefore, a gospel that has no effect in peoples' lives, which has no transforming power, is not the true or full gospel. The gospel and the coming of the Kingdom call forth conviction, compassion and courage.

Conviction

The gospel calls for a decision that each person must make and such a decision will determine the eternal destination of that person. Such a decision, when made, must bring the believer's life into conformity with the eternal truths of God, of his Son Jesus Christ, and of the Holy Spirit. God's word is truth, and every one of his righteous ordinances endures forever (Psalm 119:160). *"Jesus said to them all, 'If any want to become my followers, let them deny themselves and take up their cross daily and follow me.'"* (Luke 9:23)

This call by Jesus to all who will follow him is a call to real commitment, to conviction, as well as to consistency in following him. It is a radical decision to confront evil, sin and Satan, to change one's own way of life, and thereby to affect and to transform the lives of others. This involves self-denial: a willingness, indeed an eagerness to put other people first, putting their needs before one's own, and risking one's own life in the process. I am reminded of a young mother who, in a desperate bid to save her young child from a burning house, was terribly burned, and bore that disfigurement for the rest of her life. This is a daily business. Taking up one's cross, because that is what following Christ entails, is a way of life, for every day, with no days off. This should not surprise us, because this was the way it was for Jesus Christ, and we are claiming to follow in his footsteps.

For some converts the decision to follow Christ was indeed - and still is - a life and death issue. For example in late nineteenth century Nigeria many were tortured and suffered terribly at the hands of their pagan masters or tribesmen. Joshua Hart was a young man, one of the early converts of Bishop Samuel Ajayi Crowther, living in the town of Bonny, and his only offence was that he had renounced his idols and worshipped the living God. He attended church and refused to eat food offered to idols. For this, he was arrested and treated with great violence and cruelty, often being flung high into the air so that he would fall to the ground with great force. Despite many threats and offers of bribes, he maintained, "If my master requires me to do any work for him, however hard, I will try my best to do it. If he even requires me to carry the world itself on my head, I will try if I can do it. But if he requires me to partake of things sacrificed to the gods, I will never do it." Finally, he was bound hand and foot and thrown into the river, his head barbarously beaten by a paddle, and finally his body thrust through with a sharp pointed pole.[1]

The vast majority of Christians in the West today have not been put to this sort of test, but the choice to follow Jesus requires a conviction and commitment that go beyond mere verbal assent!

William Wilberforce (1759-1833) is remembered for his pioneering work for the abolition of slavery. From his own writings, however, his conviction is clear that attempts at political reform without changing the hearts and minds of the people are futile. Change must come from the grass roots up. He saw clearly that the big problem facing communities was "the disease of selfishness."[2] Benevolence, which is not born of Christianity, is selective in its application because its underlying motive is selfishness. When, however, the true gospel is truly heard and a person is convicted by it one of the main fruits will be compassion.

Compassion

"Jesus was moved with compassion for them, because they were weary and scattered, like sheep having no shepherd." (Mt 9:36) This is the heart of the matter in Jesus' approach to salvation. In all Scripture, the one thing that moves God to action on behalf of the poor, oppressed and lost is his compassion. It is compassion that drives action! Without compassion there will no genuine salvation action. The good Samaritan had compassion on the man beaten by robbers and he gave up the comfort

---

[1]Page, Jesse, *The Black Bishop*, Greenwood Press Connecticut, 1979, page 216

[2]Wilberforce, William, *A Practical View of Christianity*, Hendrickson USA, 1996 (reissued 2006), p.224

of being on his donkey in order to help the man; he gave his time to assist, he made money available for the health of the man and promised to settle all bills if this became necessary.

The current mission approach tends too often to look for what the mission field can provide or in fact, the missionary looks out for what he can get out of the mission field. Jesus, on the other hand, looks at the crowd and *"he had compassion on them, because they were harassed and helpless, like sheep without a shepherd."* He saw the need of the crowd, and his interest was how to solve the problem of the crowd. He also had compassion on the crowd. This is the heart of mission, for without compassion mission is impossible. It is compassion that moves the heart to act without feeling superior, and which leads to a contextualized, empathic, incarnational action. Our call to mission is a call to self-sacrifice, to give our time, talents and resources, and to show practical care and concern until the mission work is finished and completed. A mission without compassion is not likely to be in line with the mind of God! This is so because at the foot of the cross there is no favouritism. Living for Christ is living for others, for all others. It is service delivery; it is missionary; it is a total dedication and commitment to Christ and to obeying him. When there is conviction, the whole focus of life shifts from self to Christ, and if we are truly focused on Christ, then we will see the needs of the world and do something about it - with compassion.

If as Christians we desire to bring others to Christ, to establish the reign of truth and righteousness in society and finally attain everlasting life, then the only way to live is to surrender to Christ, to die to self and live to serve others. We are saved by Jesus Christ in order to serve! Those who have understood and accepted this call have changed the world in and by the power of the Holy Spirit. Through the power of the Holy Spirit, they transformed the world, and stood against injustice, evil, wickedness, diseases, poverty and inhumanity wherever such evils were found.

From my own part of Nigeria, we remember the early missionaries with immense gratitude. For example, there was the Rev. G.T. Fox, who left England for Nigeria in November 1909, and died of fever in Kano three years later, aged 31. His younger brother, a brilliant medical doctor who established the first hospital in Northern Nigeria, died when only 37. The commitment and compassion of families such as that of the Fox brothers can only be wondered at. When the father, Prebendary Fox heard that he had now lost two sons on the mission field, he offered to finance another missionary who would go out to replace his sons. Other examples of Christ-like compassion abound: Martin Luther, John Wesley, William Booth, William Wilberforce, Bishop Ajayi Crowther, Mary Slessor, Bishop Festus Kivengere, Archbishop J.A. Adetiloye, to name but a few.

Courage

At the heart of the mission of the gospel is the salvation of mankind. The work and labour of bringing freedom through the message of the gospel remains the responsibility for those who will deny self, take up the cross and follow in the footsteps of Jesus Christ. The call to mission and evangelism is the call to do exactly as Jesus Christ did. This cannot be done in our strength: Jesus will do it all through us, through the power of the Holy Spirit. This is where courage comes from.

John Wesley wrote in a letter to William Wilberforce: "Unless God has raised you up . . . you will be worn out by opposition of men and devils, but if God be for you, who can be against you? Oh be not weary of well-doing."[3]

---

[3] Wilberforce, page xiv

The cross is at the centre of the gospel; it is at the heart of the good news, the message of salvation. The cross was intended by his enemies to be the end of Jesus' ministry; it was meant to silence him by killing him. The conspiracy to kill him was completed; there was to be a supposed legal process to condemn an innocent one for opening the eyes of the blind, for lifting the down-trodden, caring for the poor, feeding the hungry and doing good. Jesus did no wrong yet the forces of envy, hatred, jealousy, bitterness, slander and betrayal condemned him. They ganged up and sentenced him to death on the cross. However, on the third day Jesus rose from the dead and is alive for evermore! On the cross he took the penalty of the sin on behalf of sinners (Rom 6:23); he died the death of sinners that we might live the life in Christ (Gal 2:20); he defeated death sin and hell and set us free!

Those who carry the message of the gospel will not always be welcomed; there may be intimidation, humiliation and suffering. St. Paul knew all of these, but he refused to give up. He searched out people of all faiths: Jews, worshippers of pagan idols, and those who served an "unknown god." Always, under all circumstances, his concern, his aim, his reason for living was to "press on" with this gospel (Phil.3:12), the gospel which had so caught and transformed him, that he knew that no one was beyond its power. Courage comes from following Jesus.

It is important to realise that such examples of the transforming power of the Holy Spirit and the resulting explosion of mission and ministry are not limited to Biblical times, nor to the early history of the church. There have been so many examples since then: suffice it to mention just a few.

William Wilberforce (1759-1833), who has already been referred to, was an English politician. In his mid-twenties he became a committed Christian and then headed the parliamentary campaign against the British slave trade for twenty-six years until the passage of the Slave Trade Act of 1807. In later years, Wilberforce supported the campaign for the complete abolition of slavery in the British Empire. Having devoted some 45 years of his life to this mission, he died just three days after hearing that the Slavery Abolition Act 1833 had been passed.

Also from England, but having a worldwide transforming effect was **Henry Venn** (1796 - 1873), an Anglican clergyman who is recognised as one of the foremost strategists of Protestant missions in the nineteenth century. He was an outstanding administrator who served as honorary secretary of the Church Missionary Society from 1841 to 1873. During his tenure of office, 498 clergymen were sent abroad, all of them passing under his inspection; with most of them, he, as secretary, maintained a regular correspondence. He was also a campaigner who frequently lobbied the British Parliament on social issues of his day, notably on ensuring the total eradication of the Atlantic Slave Trade. Venn was also influential in the life of Samuel Ajayi Crowther.

Bishop Samuel Ajayi Crowther (c.1807-1891), the first black Bishop, changed the lives of thousands as he doggedly continued with his missionary excursions, facing opposition, persecution and misunderstandings of all kinds. Having been born in Osogun, he was captured as a young boy, and taken as a slave. He was rescued and taken to Sierra Leone where he was educated. Excelling at school, he became a mission teacher and in 1841, he became a CMS representative on the Niger Mission Expedition, contributing greatly to it. He studied at the CMS College in London preparatory to ordination in 1843 – a landmark for the Anglican ministry. He was then instrumental in opening a new mission in Yorubaland, centred in Abeokuta, by that time the homeland of Crowther's Egba people. His role in translating and producing the Yoruba Bible, which set new standards for later African translations, was crucial: such translations made the gospel indigenous and long lasting. Crowther's visit to Britain in 1851 influenced government, church, and public opinion about Africa. The CMS secretary, Henry Venn, saw Crowther as a potential demonstration of the feasibility of self-governing, self-supporting, and self-propagating African churches and in 1857, Venn sent him to open a new mission on the Niger. In 1864, he was consecrated as the first black bishop and appointed as "Bishop of the countries of Western Africa beyond the Queen's dominions." His primary emphasis was always on preaching the gospel, and he was a fearless evangelist even in difficult and hostile environments. In addition, however, his work in community building, establishing congregations, developing agriculture (he brought cassava to Africa) and trade, and in pioneering an early form of Christian-Muslim dialogue, has left an indelible mark on the nation as well as on the church in Nigeria.

Rowland Bingham (1872-1942) was once heard to say, "I will open Africa to the gospel or die trying." He nearly died trying, but amid the pain of friends' deaths and against seemingly insurmountable odds, he succeeded in establishing the Sudan Interior Mission (SIM, now known as 'Serving in Mission') and bringing the Good News to the people of the Sudan. His work with SIM eventually led to the founding in 1954 of ECWA (Evangelical Church of West Africa, now called Evangelical Church Winning All).

The power of the gospel is clearly seen in the lives of these and many others like them, both those remembered and those known only to God. This same power is also seen today in the perseverance and persistence of Christians living in countries such as Northern Nigeria, Egypt, Syria, South Sudan and many others. Here is the privilege and here is the cost of living in the power of the gospel and in the power of the Holy Spirit. The Spirit is a Spirit of boldness, not of timidity and fear (2 Timothy 1:7). When the Holy Spirit was given, people began to do things that turned the world upside down, or rather, turned the world the right way up. The courage of Christians comes from the knowledge that Satan, evil, hell and death have been defeated and are powerless in the face of the cross of Christ. The Spirit gives boldness to reprove, admonish and correct. (2 Tim. 1:7). The message was clear and people understood. The power of the Spirit transforms an ordinary person into a courageous transformer so that he or she becomes not just a good, wonderful decoration in society, but a pioneer, a social reformer, a community builder, a leader, an explorer, a risk-taker, an educationalist, an honest entrepreneur, a voice for the voiceless poor, orphans, widows, oppressed and down-trodden, in order to institute and create an environment for the Kingdom of God to rule on earth now. This is what is needed today!

Conclusion

Truly to pray "Thy Kingdom Come . . .," and to live out that prayer means dying to self and living for Christ. Whenever and wherever the gospel is truly heard and lived, there will be conviction, compassion and courage. This must bring change in behaviour and character; it must bring change in health, in the environment, in education and in the economy; it must bring progress and development to people, take the lead in community life, and conduct for peace and justice. The gospel alone has the capacity to draw people of every race, tribe and nationality to live in peace and to work together in harmony for the good of all. The gospel, if it truly is the gospel that is being proclaimed, will assuredly bring life, light and growth. Because of the gospel, structures will be developed for the building of life together in communities and for the care of the environment, and at the same time, the power of the gospel will militate against all forms of dehumanization or degradation. The gospel has the cure for poverty!

This is not something in which Bishops and priests alone are to be involved! It is God's call to all Christians, young and old, educated and illiterate, rich and poor – all are called to live transformed and transforming lives, convicted, enabled, and constantly spurred on by the power of the gospel. The call to mission and evangelism is the call of God to every single Christian. The road may seem rough, the results may sometimes seem small, but one day, maybe years later, a new day will dawn and someone will say, Yes, Christ was here!

Thy Kingdom Come, O Lord.

Amen.

Now to Begin . . .

1. If you have learned anything from this book, please go and put it into practice!!

2. As a group, or as an individual, write in the space below what evangelism and Mission mean to you, and what you are going to do about it!

BIBLIOGRAPHY

Adeyemo, Tokunboh (ed.). *Africa Bible Commentary*. Nairobi: Zondervan/ World Alive Publishers, 2006.

Akanni, Gbile. *What God Looks for in his Vessel*. Gboko: Peace House Publications, 1999.

Barclay, William. *The Daily Study Bible: The Acts of the Apostles*. Edinburgh: The Saint Andrew Press, 2003.

Braaten, Carl E. *The Apostolic Imperative*. Minneapolis: Augsburg Press, 1985.

Bucer, Martin. *Concerning the True Care of Souls*. Edinburgh: Banner of Truth Trust, 2009.

Carden, John (ed.). *Morning, Noon and Night, Prayers and Meditations from the Third World*. London: CMS, 1976.

Church of Nigeria (Anglican Communion). *The Book of Common Prayer*. reprinted. Lagos: CSS, 2002.

Fitch, David E. *The Great Giveaway: Reclaiming the Mission of the Church from Big Business, Parachurch Organizations, Psychotherapy, Consumer Capitalism, and Other Modern Maladies*. Grand Rapids: Baker Books, 2005.

Gillard, Richard A.M. *Scripture in Song*. (a division of Integrity Music Inc), 1977.

Green, Michael. *Evangelism Through the Local Church*. London: Hodder and Stoughton, 1991.

Latourette, Kenneth Scott. *The First Five Centuries, vol. 1 of A History of the Expansion of Christianity*. New York: Harper and Bros., 1937.

Neill, Stephen. *A History of Christian Missions*. London: Pelican Books, 1964.

Newbigin, Lesslie. *The Open Secret: An Introduction to the Theology of Mission*. rev. ed. Grand Rapids: Eerdmans, 1995.

Null, Ashley. *Thomas Cranmer's Doctrine of Repentance*. Oxford: Oxford University Press, 2000.

Orombi, Henry Luke. *What Is Anglicanism?*. 2007. Available http://www.firstthings.com/article/2007/08/001-what-is-anglicanism.

Osei-Mensah, G. *Wanted: Servant Leaders: The Challenge of Christian Leadership in Africa Today*. Africa Christian Press, 1990. Theological Perspectives in Africa No.3.

Page, Jesse. *The Black Bishop*. Westport: Greenwood Press, 1979.

Pilavachi, Mike. *When Necessary Use Words: Changing Lives Through Justice and Evangelism*. Minneapolis: Bethany House Publishers, 2006.

Ryle, JC. *Knots Untied*. Moscow: Charles Nolan Publishers, 2000.

Scudieri, Robert J. *The Apostolic Church: One, Holy, Catholic, and Missionary*. Chino: Lutheran Society for Missiology, 1995.

Magdalene, Sister Margaret. *Jesus Man of Prayer*. London: Hodder & Stoughton, 1987.

Stott, J.W.R. *The Message of Acts: To the Ends of the Earth*. Nottingham: I.V.P., 1990.

The Book of Common Prayer. New York: Church Pension Fund, 1986.

Weldon, Glen and Robertson, Earl. *Prayer in Evangelism, Lausanne Occasional Paper No. 42,*. Lausanne Committee for World Evangelization, 2005. Available https://www.lausanne.org/wp-content/uploads/2007/06/LOP42_IG13.pdf.

Wilberforce, William. *A Practical View of Christianity*. reissued. Peabody: Hendrickson, 2006.

Wright, Chistopher J. H. *The Mission of God's People*. Grand Rapids: Zondervan, 2010.

9 789897 890538 03